Restructuring American Corporations

Restructuring American Corporations

CAUSES, EFFECTS, AND IMPLICATIONS

Abbass F. Alkhafaji

Q

QUORUM BOOKS

New York • Westport, Connecticut • London

Library of Congress Cataloging-in-Publication Data

Alkhafaji, Abbass F.
   Restructuring American corporations : causes, effects, and
implications / Abbass F. Alkhafaji.
      p. cm.
   Includes bibliographical references.
   ISBN 0-89930-573-3 (lib. bdg. : alk. paper)
      1. Consolidation and merger of corporations—United States.
   2. Corporate reorganizations—United States.   I. Title.
   HD2746.5.A38   1990
   338.8'3'0973—dc20   90-32699

British Library Cataloguing in Publication Data is available.

Library of Congress Catalog Card Number: 90-32699
ISBN: 0-89930-573-3

First published in 1990

Quorum Books, 88 Post Road West, Westport, CT 06881
An imprint of Greenwood Publishing Group, Inc.

Printed in the United States of America

The paper used in this book complies with the
Permanent Paper Standard issued by the National
Information Standards Organization (Z39.48–1984).

10 9 8 7 6 5 4 3 2 1

CONTENTS

TABLES AND FIGURES

TABLES

FIGURES

PREFACE

Mergers, acquisitions, and takeovers are nothing new to American businesses. The huge dollar amounts involved in buyouts, however, is a new aspect of this game. Large corporations that were once thought to be safe from any takeover attempts are now potential targets for big-money investors. In addition, the number of mergers, acquisitions, and takeovers has increased dramatically in recent years.

This book explores the reasons for the increasing popularity of takeovers, mergers, and buyouts. In addition it examines the issues of beneficiaries and losers in takeovers, the international aspects of buyouts, and future implications of buyouts for managers.

More specifically, the objectives of this book are:

1. To provide a historical perspective on mergers, takeovers, and buyouts and a rationale for their rapid increase
2. To explain the various characteristics of companies that prompt mergers, takeovers, and buyouts, as well as their short- and long-term implications
3. To discuss the impact of restructuring on the economy
4. To highlight the future of restructuring
5. To investigate the implications of this phenomenon
6. To devise a comprehensive and practical guide to the restructuring which typically follows mergers, takeovers, and buyouts

7. To explain the various stages of mergers, takeovers, and buyouts to help
   future managers understand these relatively new phenomena
8. To show why buyouts have become popular in the international marketplace

These topics are discussed comprehensively but simply. The discussion includes an extensive review of the available literature with real world examples. It also includes some of the author's empirical studies on management's perception of this issue. Its impact on the economy, trends, government regulation, and managerial implications will be discussed as well. The topics are current and have not yet been covered extensively in most published texts.

This book will be useful for today's managers as well as future managers. It will help professionals understand the phenomenon of restructuring and show how they can prepare for the future.

ACKNOWLEDGMENTS

This book would have been impossible without the help of numerous friends, colleagues, and students. Among the friends who gave encouragement and insightful advice are Dr. Rogene Buchholz, Dr. Raymond Lutz, Dr. Mike Ross, Dr. Glenn Robinson, Dr. Abbas Ali, Dr. Matt Gibbs, Dr. Robert Camp, Dr. Richard Judy, Dr. Rauf Khan, Dr. Mohammad Alhadi, Dr. Abo Habib, Dr. Daniel Twomey, Dr. Ron Sardessai, and Dr. Galal Elhagrasey.

I am grateful to several students who reviewed some of the chapters and provided valuable comments. Some also provided valuable support in the form of typing—Tod Bryant, Jodi Debaker, and Pam Brager—and editorial assistance—Judy Clare, Jani ann McWreath, Elizabeth Wright, Robert Jones, Eric Crawford, Lori Meehan, Charles Rinaman, Nafeesa Essof, Mohammed Zubair Afaq, Khozaim Zanzibar, and Keith Douglas McMillan.

I extend my thanks to all of my students in my management seminars and Environmental Issues in Management course for their continuous support. Special thanks to Dr. Frank Mastrianna and all my colleagues in the department of management and marketing at Slippery Rock University for their encouragement and support in this endeavor. Of course, the responsibility for any error or omission lies only with the author.

My special thanks and appreciation go to my loving family for their support and for giving me the inspiration and strength to write this book. This book is dedicated to my dearest father and mother and my beautiful daughters, Alliah and Sheamah, whom I love and I miss very much. This book is also dedicated to my wife for her support and understanding.

1

THE BUYOUT PHENOMENON

The main reasons investors such as Kohlberg, Kravis, & Roberts and Drexel, Burnham Lambert, Inc., buy out large corporations are the large amounts of short-term money that can be made and the tax advantages that result. Stockholders, investment bankers, and high-level management also stand to benefit from a buyout. These facts have led to a dramatic increase in the number of buyouts in recent years.

There is, however, a negative aspect to the buyout phenomenon the United States is currently experiencing. The tax advantages of buyouts ultimately become a burden to the individual, creating more problems for society as a whole. In addition, mergers, takeovers, and buyouts are allowing investors to restructure corporate America. This strikes fear in the heart of average Americans concerned about job security.

American blue-collar workers need to worry about their jobs; however, lower-, middle-, and top-level managers' jobs could be on the line as a result of corporate restructuring as well. This possibility implies that current and future managers should be concerned about the implications of the many buyouts that have taken place, are currently taking place, and will continue to take place unless something is done to control them. If nothing is done managers will have to be more diligent in monitoring the corporate environment.

Although the popularity and frequency of buyouts are on the rise, many oppose hostile buyouts and are trying to curb such occurrences. One such individual attempting to curb takeovers and buyouts is Senator Lloyd Bentson of Texas. Bentson is attempting to develop a formula which will reduce the amount of tax incentives companies receive as a result of being bought out. This reduction will eliminate one of the major benefits of going from public to private after a buyout.

Another reason Bentson and others oppose today's inordinate number of takeovers is because the emphasis on making huge sums of money in the short run tends to lose sight of long-term goals. Investing in research and development and new equipment is not a priority among most investors. This can severely inhibit the productivity of a company which needs to reinvest in order to remain competitive.

THE EFFECTS OF CORPORATE RESTRUCTURING ON SOCIETY

From a social point of view, takeovers create genuine suffering for individuals whose jobs are eliminated or whose lifelong careers are ruined; entire communities can experience abrupt economic dislocation. A corporation is a sociological institution as well as a collection of financial assets. While employees understand that corporate change is necessary to corporate survival, they will not accept abrupt, radical change imposed from outside that has nothing to do with current business conditions.[1]

Politicians are also unlikely to accept the current takeover craze. Already antitakeover laws are being passed at the state level, and it is only a matter of time before Congress intervenes. The Supreme Court handed down an important securities law decision in March 1988, designed to protect investors from stock manipulation. The law prohibits a public company from making untrue, misleading, or incomplete statements about facts that are "material" to its fortunes. Companies must disclose merger talks immediately rather than waiting until such talks reach fruition. A wrong move can invite challenges from the Securities and Exchange Commission (SEC) and from stockholders who say they were misled. Because shareholder lawsuits are often brought as class actions, the potential damages could amount to millions of dollars.[2]

Legislation that has been passed to restrict takeovers has been relatively ineffective. Those who support takeovers argue that such laws favor existing management no matter how inefficient or self-serving. The board of directors can hardly be expected to rectify this situation; it was chosen by management and will challenge or dismiss management only in the most extreme situations. Problems posed by ineffectual or self-serving management should be addressed in a manner that keeps politicians out of the process. Stockholders need protection from this type of management; workers, executives, and communities need protection from corporate dismemberment.

The concepts of stockholder and stockholder rights need to be redefined. The main reason that hostile takeovers are relatively easy is that by the time the rumor mill has spread the word and the price of the stock has soared, a substantial portion of that stock will be in the hands of arbitrageurs. Arbitrageurs are not stockholders in the classic sense but merely speculators. They have no interest in the corporation as an institution, feel neither affection nor loyalty to the institution, and are active only in the hope of quick profit. They should not have a decisive voice in determining the future of the institution; there is no reason for them to have a voice at all. No stockholder should be entitled to a vote unless and until he has held the stock for one year. Such a residency requirement, while not prohibiting takeovers, would prevent corporations from being easy targets and would not allow management to perpetuate itself regardless of performance. If a majority of stockholders were intensely dissatisfied with management, a proxy fight could well result in its ouster.

THE LBO CRAZE

LBOs—leveraged buyouts—are the hottest craze in finance, both in the United States and abroad. If a company has gone private in the last several years, chances are good that it did so through an LBO. In 1989 Days Inn Corp., Safeways Inc., Atlantic A Plus minimarkets and gas stations on the East Coast, and bathroom fixture maker American Standard have been taken over, borrowing huge sums in order to buy out shareholders. The largest LBO in 1988 was Montgomery Ward at $3.8 billion; Kroger Co. has been threatened by Kohlberg, Kravis, & Roberts with a $4.6-billion LBO.

These deals are highly profitable because the stock prices of many companies do not reflect the value of their assets. An investor group, frequently led by company management, decides to buy the company from shareholders. To fund the deal, the investors borrow up to 90 percent of the money needed, pledging the company's assets as collateral. Using this leverage to take the company private, investors can sell off subsidiaries and streamline what is left, slashing jobs and reducing overhead. Ideally, the debt is paid back within four years and the investors are left with a smaller, well-focused business.

Firms go private to avoid hostile takeovers or because management is tired of low stock prices. Profits can be enormous but if the economy goes into recession, there will be few bidders for the assets LBO firms must sell. If investors fail to make operations leaner or more profitable, or obtain the price they expect for assets, the debt may destroy them, as in the case of Revco, a 1986 LBO. The borrowed money comes not only from Wall Street speculators, but from banks, insurance firms, pension funds, and so on. At this time, an estimated $25 billion is set aside to initiate LBOs; leveraged at 10 to 1, this amounts to $250 billion in purchasing power.[3]

Mergers differ from takeovers in that a joint decision to combine two companies is made with the mutual agreement of both. Firms merge with the goal of becoming more diverse, gaining market share, or penetrating new markets. The recent burst of takeover mania involving food and brand-name consumer products is reminiscent of the oil company merger craze of the early 1980s. Buyers see value in these companies, with their potential for economy of scale in global production, marketing, and distribution. They see nothing wrong with the astounding prices being offered, such as the $25.3-billion bid by Kohlberg, Kravis, & Roberts for RJR Nabisco. Do these brand-name takeovers make sense and will they work, or will they fail spectacularly if the debt-ridden buyers suddenly find themselves facing a recession?

From 1981 to 1984, with oil prices at $30 a barrel, oil companies pursued each other with abandon, only to witness the price of oil plunge to $10 a barrel in 1986. However, analysts say that the brand-names in the latest proposals are so powerful that the firms involved need not worry about failing. Companies which borrowed heavily to swing these deals could face other problems. Their flexibility is reduced even if interest rates remain stable, because there is no cash left over for reinvestment in brand-names. If a competitor that is unencumbered by such huge debt decides to wage a marketing war, a brand may be unable to respond, leading to the loss of customers. Certain fixed costs must be paid, regardless of the level of production, so even a small drop in sales can cause a sizable drop in profits.

The most immediate problem stemming from many mergers—besides pink slips going to employees—is their staggering cost. The need to quickly reduce debt contributes to the pursuit of short-term goals at the expense of long-term competitiveness. In an effort to save money and jobs, management may skimp on research and development (R&D); competitors may surpass them, as in the case of the U.S. steel industry.

Effects of mergers on the workforce extend beyond those who suddenly find themselves unemployed. Fear created among executives may encourage them to secure excess compensation, resulting in cynicism all the way down the corporate ladder. Morale can suffer if companies, subsidiaries, and employees are shifted around; staff reductions will create stiffer competition for managerial jobs.

THE ECONOMIC IMPORTANCE OF RESTRUCTURING

The implications of the merger craze for the economy and society are even more disturbing. First, it makes the economy more vulnerable to bad decisions made by a declining number of top executives; mistakes made by large companies effect the economy more than those made by small firms. Top-level management now spends more time and money trying to prevent their companies from being taken over than they spend worrying about the quality of their product and how it can be distributed more efficiently.

Second, talented students are being lost to professions such as law and finance because of the high salaries that these fields offer. The number of students graduating with engineering degrees has decreased over the past few years, which will hurt our economy in the long run.

Third, the merger craze tends to enlarge the role of government, as evidenced by the special favors to corporations included in the current trade bill. In the event of a recession, populist demand for regulation of the economy will increase.

Fourth, the merger craze gives a foreign company buying into U.S. industry the opportunity to snap up a larger chunk at one time. Such threats encourage protectionism, to the detriment of the economy. The United States will not be able to compete with foreign countries when it comes to research and development of new products.

Studies by the National Science Foundation show that R&D is the first area where spending is cut during a buyout. Sixteen companies that had undergone mergers showed a 4.7 percent drop in R&D spending. Eight companies may be eliminating duplication and inefficiencies. If this is the case, the public will benefit as research becomes more defined and costs are reduced resulting in a better product at a lower price. Alfred Rappaport, a professor at Northwestern University's Kellogg School of Management specializing in mergers and acquisitions, argues that most leveraged buyouts do not include high-tech or research-oriented businesses.

For example, after being sold off to a management-led buyout from EXXON, Reliance Electric reduced its R&D spending from $30 million to $25 million and is actually investing more toward being competitive with products tailor-made to specific customers. Reliance vice-president Peter Tsivitse claims that the company is "executing projects faster, more efficiently and experiencing less waste since the buyout."[4] Reliance, due to the turnaround in R&D, has received a contract to make a twenty-first-century electric motor using the newest superconductors.

Finally, restructuring puts intense pressure on those who stay on the job. It seems like one group's gain is another one's loss. Without trust people will not dedicate themselves to common goals, but invest their energy in defending their own interests, which means declining productivity.

For all the dangers, the surge in mergers may do some good. Many companies, forced to reduce debt rapidly, become more efficient. As companies concentrate their efforts on fewer businesses, the economy may benefit. However, all too many mergers are simply pointless exercises in rearranging the economic landscape.

NOTES

1. Henry F. Myers, "Will Mergers Help or Hurt in the Long Run?" *Wall Street Journal* (May 2, 1988).

2. Wayne E. Green, "Confusion over Merger-Disclosure Law," *Wall Street Journal* (June 24, 1988).

3. Daniel Kadle, "Buyout Craze May Be Too Good to Last," *USA Today* (September 30, 1988).

4. Anthony Ramirez, "What LBOs Really Do to R&D Spending," *Fortune* (March 1989): 98.

2

THE NEW ENTREPRENEUR

Recent literature on entrepreneurship has expanded the focus from new ventures to ongoing enterprises in various stages of development. There are several types of entrepreneurs, some craftsmen and others opportunistic, some working alone and others in "smart teams" such as the founders of Compaq Computer. This chapter presents a model of entrepreneurship which integrates entrepreneurial activities with the entrepreneurial environment. This approach helps explain why entrepreneurs thrive in more turbulent environments than other individuals.

DEFINITION

An entrepreneur can be defined in many ways. One definition focuses on the activity by which an individual enters a new business. Another definition involves the first stage of the corporate life-cycle. An entrepreneur may develop and design a corporation. After the initial stage of this company, the entrepreneur may be replaced by an individual who will design the later stages of the corporation. Entrepreneurs may establish themselves in new areas through another means—namely, by restructuring existing companies emphasizing the strategic changes.

Peter Drucker defines an entrepreneur as "somebody who endows resources with new wealth-producing capacity."[1] He also emphasizes that a small business is not necessarily an entrepreneurial business. Many small businesses do not have the resources, time, or ambition to be entrepreneurial.

CHARACTERISTICS

Studies have identified a number of characteristics which are common to successful entrepreneurs. This is especially important in the case of young corporations, because the entrepreneur and the organization are often virtually synonymous.

The first characteristic is high achievement motivation. The successful entrepreneur works long hours and dislikes inefficiency. This characteristic often describes not only originators of entrepreneurial companies but managers who play an entrepreneurial role.

A second characteristic is the ability to be enterprising. The successful entrepreneur is a good leader, as opposed to a good follower or subordinate. This person usually needs little support or encouragement from others.

A third characteristic is the presence of a large amount of stress with its consequences. The symptoms of stress are headaches, digestive problems, and sleeplessness. This stress is usually present regardless of the individual's success or failure.

The last characteristic which is emphasized by Drucker is work experience in a large organization. "The most successful of the young entrepreneurs today are people who have spent five to eight years in a large organization."[2] Through this experience the entrepreneur will learn the art of analysis, training procedures, the delegation of authority, and how to encourage teamwork.

The style of an entrepreneur and the organization is not similar in most cases. In addition there is a wide range of policies and strategies used by these individuals and their organizations. Generally, entrepreneurs can be divided into two groups, the craftsmen and the opportunistics.

The craftsman entrepreneur tends to be educated and trained in one specific area, unaware of or unconcerned with the social environment. This type of entrepreneur will introduce a minimal amount of change in a company and will envision minimal future growth. This individual will usually work for a fairly rigid firm.

The opportunistic entrepreneur tends to have a well-rounded education and is familiar with and confident in social interaction. This person is aware of and anticipates the future. This type of entrepreneur tends to supervise change and diversification in a firm. An opportunistic entrepreneur will be part of an adaptive firm.

Many entrepreneurs establish themselves by building a new business from scratch and working to remain solvent and to earn a profit. However, there is another kind of entrepreneur who acquires an established business. This process is known as entrepreneurial leveraged buyout (E-LBO). An E-LBO involves the buying out of a company whose profits are known whereas the establishment of a new company involves a much higher risk. The financing of both, however, is a major concern.

Institutions are willing to help finance E-LBOs due to the fact that the risk is much lower than the financing of new ventures. Institutional lenders are aware of the fact that entrepreneurs are likely to be educated and knowledgeable about the field into which they are buying. Also, major investors are likely to be wealthy, thus reinforcing their success as entrepreneurs and reassuring the lender. An institutional lender feels safer about investing his money in an E-LBO when the entrepreneur himself is making a large contribution. Lending companies may seek to secure loans with personal guarantees, however, especially when the amount is substantial.

Institutional lenders are likely to provide long repayment periods. This is due to the confidence that lenders have in E-LBOs. They do not feel a need to demand the money in a short period of time because the company is unlikely to have any great cash flow in the initial stages. In this way, leverage financers earn more interest over the longer repayment period.

Institutional lenders charge much lower interest rates to E-LBOs than to nonentrepreneurial LBO investors. This is because lenders are confident in stable industries, established companies, and respected investors.

COMPAQ COMPUTER

One of the hottest entrepreneurs in America today is the "smart team" of Compaq Computer. This company was founded by Bill Murto, Jim Harris, and Rod Canion. All were senior managers at Texas Instruments Inc. This team decided to develop a portable personal computer that was compatible with the IBM PC. Not only was this decision successful, but the way the team set its strategy was also considered appropriate. In four years Compaq has become the world's second largest manufacturer of personal computers for business. Their 1985 sales came close to a half-billion dollars.

As opposed to the one-man show, this company was formed as a team without resting on the capabilities of one man. Rod Canion, the president, does not regard himself as a superstar with all the vision, but as an individual who moderates a consensus among a group of competent people. This smart team has decided against the strategy of making quick money. Instead, they focus on the goal of building a company that is going to last. This idea of building a management team is not unique. Many high-tech CEOs were asked to identify their top priority in running a business. Two-thirds agreed that the development of a strong management team was most important. A company can no longer simply sell a high-tech item; the item has to be made well and marketed well, and all business aspects must be considered.

The founders of Compaq wanted to create a company that combined the discipline of a large company with the participative environment of a smaller company. This "smart team" used an interdisciplinary approach to management. The treasurer, engineer, and marketing manager together make the best possible decision about manufacturing. This was the way top management made their decision and this process was implemented throughout the company.

It is easy to see how Compaq moved into a market niche with a new product in ninety days. This niche was created by IBM for super PCs. Compaq quickly gained control of this niche and received with it 3 to 4 percent more of the business-computer market—all because of teamwork.

Compaq has consistently led the industry with products that incorporate the latest technology. Once Compaq commits itself to a product, work on all aspects of it is undertaken simultaneously. According to Canion, Compaq strives to compress the process into a six- to nine-month period rather than the more typical twelve to eighteen months. For instance, when IBM unveiled its PC, Compaq was one of several dozen startups that jumped into the market with comparable products. Compaq became a master of "creative imitation, or entrepreneurial judo."[3]

Compaq's founders discovered some ways by which they could stand out from the crowd. One was their now famous portable computer, which was an instant hit. The second decision was to develop strong relationships with computer retailers (which was a new concept in the industry). From the beginning, Compaq realized that retailers were the key and that store shelf space would become scarce. Compaq won the battle; today one in every six personal computers sold by dealers are made by Compaq.

John Gribi, senior vice-president of finance, notes that even in the beginning Compaq was a "large company in its formative stages, not a small company trying to grow big."[4] Compaq has been successful through the years by relying on their slogan, "doing what makes sense."

Probably the main reason Compaq was an instant success is because of management's attitude and ideas. Canion notes that one of the things that makes him feel good about his job is the fulfillment that people get out of going after tough projects and working hard as a team to overcome the obstacles. John C. Dean, a senior analyst with San Francisco-based Montgomery Securities, attributes a large portion of Compaq's positive reputation with dealers to "Canion's ability to deal openly and honestly with the outside world."[5]

Sales ending March 31, 1988, had gone up 108 percent, with a sharp increase in international sales and good acceptance of new products. The revenues for the year 1988 were projected to grow 40 percent, aided by strong demand for personal computers and increased penetration of the international market. Compaq intends to continue to invest heavily in research and marketing. In 1987, net sales reached a little over $1.2 billion, a dramatic increase from the $625 million earned in 1986. The increase in total assets from 1986 to 1987 was drastic. The company recorded $378 million in assets in 1986 and a remarkable $901 million in assets in 1987. And sales are not about to level off.

Compaq's success is due to its entrepreneurial leader and the innovative managerial staff. Canion believes in a humanistic approach to management, listening to and encouraging questions from his subordinates. Compaq also combines research and manufacturing stages in order to enter the market before competitors. Compaq sales will doubtless continue to rise steadily due to high-tech products which are closing the gap between IBM and itself.

The proper goal of the new entrepreneur is building a company that lasts, an economic institution that endures. The idea is not how strong a company is in five years, but how strong it will be in twenty-five years, and this requires teamwork.[6]

CHANGING CORPORATE STRATEGIES

Being an entrepreneur means being creative, independent, and coming up with ideas before others do. A successful entrepreneur is first in the market and consistently improving. It may seem that entrepreneurs in small businesses have an advantage over large businesses because they do not have to go through all of the complicated channels that exist in large businesses. However, things are changing because large businesses realize that change is necessary in order to maintain the competitive edge. Large businesses realize that expansion into new markets is dominated by small businesses. So how do large businesses react?

Campbell's president R. Gordon McGovern believes that large companies have to think like small companies in order to be innovative. This is necessary for diversification and expansion into smaller niches that-are dominated by small businesses. However, the major problem begins when market shares of dominant products fall due to innovative new products and ideas that are catching people's eyes. Consumers are more health-conscious and are willing to try new products. Campbell's market was declining because it was not innovative. McGovern responded by breaking Campbell down into some fifty independent business units, giving each a charter to develop its own products. This allowed for less complicated channels and greater creativity. Each business unit has its own general manager who, as effective chief executive officer, has under him a marketing director, controller, and product development staff.

Because large businesses are starting to think like small businesses, and small businesses lack resources, small businesses can be bought out. How can small businesses protect themselves from takeover or failure due to imitation by larger companies? There are four ways to fight giants.

One way is to not play ball by big league rules. For example, small businesses should not get involved in a price war with large corporations, because the latter can hold out longer. The best way for a small company to fight off a price war is to maintain its market or loyal customers and keep them happy. This is what happened with Vlasic and Farman's in Seattle. Vlasic priced their pickles at a very competitive price, much lower than Farman's. But customers remained loyal due to their belief in quality and Farman's established reputation. Had Farman's tried to compete in the price war, they would have priced themselves out of the market totally. Thus Farman's maintained 60 percent of the pickle business in Seattle.

The second way is to hit large companies "where they ain't." This means finding niches in the market and establishing a reputation. A small business must establish loyal customers before large companies arrive.

Another way is for a small company to innovate, and innovate again. It takes longer for large companies to make decisions and go through all the proper channels. If large companies are involved with the same product, another innovation technique is necessary. Innovate and create again. This way the market changes more quickly than the big companies.

The fourth way to compete with giants is to build a better mousetrap. If the giant hits the market before the smaller company, the smaller company has to improve on the same product. By creating a better product before the leading manufacturer, one can recapture the market.

However, large companies are catching on to small business strategies. Campbell's has changed its business strategy by breaking the company into fifty business units instead of one. With this kind of thinking, small companies have to come up with even better and more creative ideas. That is why they are run by entrepreneurs.

THE NEW ENTREPRENEUR

In 1963, Joseph Hamilton founded Texfi Industries, Inc., to make polyester double knits. At the time, polyester double knits were extremely popular. Hamilton was confident that the product had a bright future, and so he invested $40 million in two manufacturing plants that allowed him to sidestep polyester suppliers. By the mid-1970s, however, the double knit phase had ended and the plants were an albatross around Hamilton's neck. The once successful company began to lose money, and lenders withdrew credit lines. Faced with bankruptcy, in 1980 the board recruited L. Terrell Sovey, an experienced veteran of textile management with Milliken and Lowenstein. Since the deal meant sharing power with Hamilton, Sovey refused the offer; however, he did agree to join Texfi's board on a part-time advisory basis. The board heeded his advice, selling off double knit pants, slashing management staff, and trimming back on luxury items. Within a year Texfi was out of the red.[7]

As Sovey gained the board's confidence, Hamilton's influence decreased. In 1982, Hamilton stunned the board by announcing that he had a buyer for the company. The buyout fell through at about the same time as the 1982 recession hit. Texfi once again suffered huge losses, and once again the specter of bankruptcy loomed on the horizon. Hamilton, ready to throw in the towel, shopped around for another buyer. One of the board members, impressed with Sovey's track record, secretly asked Sovey if he would be willing to take over Texfi's reins with the proviso that Hamilton retire.

It was at this point that Sovey emerged as a "new" entrepreneur. So confident was he in his ability, that not only was he willing to become chairman and chief executive, but he was willing to do so with no pay for a year. Sovey was willing to take such a risk because part of his consulting fees over the previous four years were options on one hundred thousand shares of stock. If Hamilton sold the ailing company, Sovey's options would have been worthless. Only by putting Texfi back in a profitable situation would these options pay off. The risks were great, but so was the opportunity for reward.

And so began Texfi's rapid rise. "Once in charge, Sovey scrutinized every expense, from Texfi's pension plan to its Federal Express bills."[8] He closed luxury corporate headquarters and moved them into the plant; he cut the corporate staff from one hundred to four; he raised money, slashed debt, negotiated new lines of credit, and closed old plants. Within a year, Texfi was once again breaking even.

With huge tax-loss carryforwards, Sovey moved the company from its contraction phase into one of expansion. He shopped for new businesses, targeting only those with a minimum 20 percent return on assets.

The growth was financed with $25 million raised by issuing preferred shares of stock. "Now Texfi is in a wide range of new niche businesses—making everything from narrow elastic fabrics and mapholders for General Motors to mattress ticking for state prisons and yarn for underwear and sweatclothes."[9] Other acquisitions include a fleecewear firm and a T-shirt manufacturer. So unlike Hamilton, who was stuck with polyester double knits when they were no longer in fashion, Sovey has cushioned Texfi against fashion fads and fluctuations. As Alyssa A. Lappen notes, "when one product goes soft, others should pick up the slack."[10]

Sovey has moved Texfi from a position of heavy losses to one of sales over $300 million, with an aftertax return of over 5 percent—one and a half times the industry median.[11] Stock that in 1984 was worth only $1.50 a share now sells for $11. Since exercising his stock options in 1986, Sovey's shares are now worth over $4 million.

Sovey's knowledge of both the industry and the market, his financial acumen, his dynamic management style, his ability to make tough decisions, his willingness to take risks, and his strategy for the long haul truly show him to be a "new" entrepreneur—not necessarily one who starts a business from scratch, but one who can pick an ailing company up by its bootstraps and, once again, make it a viable contributor to the economy.

THE ENTREPRENEURIAL ENVIRONMENT

Why do entrepreneurs seem to thrive under stressful conditions that others would find difficult or impossible to handle? What causes the "entrepreneurial spirit"?

An analysis of the four characteristics of entrepreneurs (high achievement motivation, good leadership, high stress, and work experience) and the two types of entrepreneur (opportunistic and adaptive) can help in answering these questions.

The first two characteristics—achievement motivation and leadership—are internal qualities of the entrepreneur. A highly motivated person seeks challenges and is willing to risk failure to gain a chance for success.[12] A good leader creates conditions in which his or her subordinates can also succeed at their jobs.

The remaining two characteristics—stress and work experience—are aspects of the entrepreneur's environment. They result from the demanding, turbulent conditions of modern business. Figure 2.1 shows the interactions between entrepreneurial qualities and the entrepreneurial environment.

The entrepreneur, being a highly motivated leader, creates and/or chooses the challenging, stressful entrepreneurial environment which

Figure 2.1
Interactions Between Entrepreneurial Qualities and the Entrepreneurial
Environment

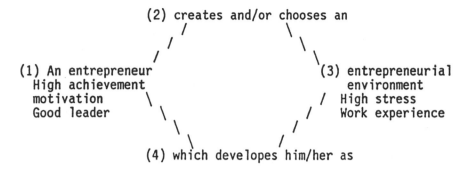

develops his or her motivational and leadership traits. This cycle will continue, so that the entrepreneur will become even more "entrepreneurial," capable of leading and thriving in environments that generate more and more challenge and stress.

The example of Compaq Computer illustrates this cycle. A "smart team" of entrepreneurs were achievement-motivated leaders who created an organization which reflects their personal drive and vision. This organization, in turn, by fostering creativity in a participative climate, will develop and reinforce entrepreneurial achievement motivation and leadership effectiveness.

ENTREPRENEURIAL ACTIVATION

Entrepreneurs seek out and thrive in an environment that is more stimulating and challenging than the norm. "Activation theory," which plots the relationship between stimulation and performance, can provide the framework for a better understanding of this process.[13]

Activation theory states that organisms are subjected to environmental stimulation which arouses them to various degrees. The greater the level of environmental stimulation, the higher will be the organism's arousal level. Either too little or too much stimulation will not arouse the organism to perform a task effectively. Too little stimulation does not provide enough incentive, while too much causes anxiety and counterproductive behavior. For example, a supervisor may place either too few or too many demands on a subordinate. Too few, and the subordinate becomes complacent; too many, and he suffers from "burnout." The relationship between arousal level and performance is shown in figure 2.2.

Figure 2.2
Arousal Level and Performance

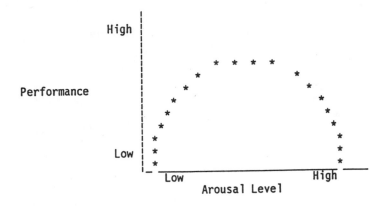

Figure 2.3
Performance of Nonentrepreneurs, Craftsmen Entrepreneurs, and Opportunistic Entrepreneurs as a Function of Arousal Level

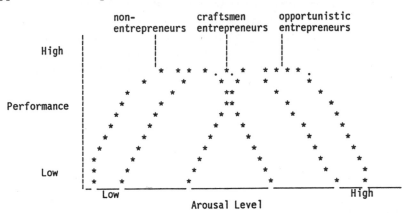

Entrepreneurs can adapt to higher levels of stimulation than others. This is because of the interaction between their personal qualities and their environment. Furthermore, some entrepreneurs—the opportunistic kind—seem especially capable of handling stress and change. Unlike craftsmen entrepreneurs, who work for more rigid firms, opportunistic entrepreneurs seek change and adaptation. Figure 2.3 compares the performance of nonentrepreneurs, craftsmen entrepreneurs, and opportunistic entrepreneurs as a function of arousal level.

In conclusion, we all perform best when aroused by our environment to the proper degree. For entrepreneurs, especially the opportunistic kind, the optimal level of environmental stimulation is higher than for others. Thus, they seek out and thrive in the highly successful, risky, challenging entrepreneurial environment. This is their "entrepreneurial spirit."

CONCLUSION

The emerging view of entrepreneurship described in this chapter reflects changes that have taken place in the individuals, organizations, and environmental conditions of our society. Individuals, through a variety of workshops, courses, books, and the like, are encouraged to think like entrepreneurs, to develop their achievement motivation levels, and to lead with vision and courage. Organizations such as Compaq Computers are providing the supportive, participative, decentralized conditions conducive to entrepreneurship. As environmental change, stress, and uncertainty increase in our society, there must be a corresponding expansion of the concept of entrepreneurship and research on its impact.

NOTES

1. Tom Richman, "The Entrepreneurial Mystique," *INC* (October 1985): 36.
2. Ibid.
3. Stuart Gannes, "America's Fastest-Growing Companies," *Fortune* (May 23, 1988): 28–31.
4. Ibid., p. 32.
5. Karen Berney, "A Reason by any Other Name," *Nation's Business* (May 1988): 45.
6. Joel Kotkin, "The Smart Team at Compaq Computer," *INC* (February 1986): 48–56.
7. Alyssa A. Lappen, "Scuffle in the Boardroom," *Forbes* (October 16, 1989): 112.
8. Ibid., p. 116.
9. Ibid.
10. Ibid.
11. Ibid., p. 112.
12. David McClelland, *The Achieving Society* (Princeton, N.J.: Van Nostrand, 1961).
13. Elizabeth Duffy, *Activation and Behavior* (New York: Wiley, 1962).

3

CORPORATE MERGERS

Mergers and acquisitions are changing the face of large businesses in the United States. The term *merger* refers to the situation in which two companies harmoniously form one corporation. Mergers differ from takeovers in that during a takeover there is little or no concern for the target company. In a merger, the companies work together to achieve the best for both. Perhaps the wave of mergers in America today springs from motives of corporate managers, convinced by financial wizards that they can be more successful together than separately.

It is important to distinguish between mergers, aquisitions, and takeovers. A merger is a friendly or voluntary combination of two or more companies. A takeover usually means the acquisition of control through stock purchase without the agreement of the directors of the company. "An acquisition is any transaction in which a buyer acquires all or part of the assets and business of a seller, or all or part of the stock or other securities of the seller, where the transaction is closed between a willing buyer and a willing seller."[1]

There are many reasons why businesses combine. A compelling one is to decrease competition. If two companies merge they no longer have to compete against each other, and it also gives the merging companies the ability to compete more effectively with larger companies in the business. "From an accounting view, mergers and acquisitions are also undertaken in order to obtain the economies of size, such as quantity discounts, concentrated selling efforts, and lower cost due to volume."[2] From a management perspective, companies combine because of simplicity of title transfers and an opportunity for a charter amendment. And one final reason for combining companies is the fact that many companies can consolidate expenses. For example, advertising for one large firm is cheaper than advertising for two smaller firms.

THE HISTORY OF MERGERS

Mergers and acquisitions began many years ago. In the 1860s, many companies merged in order to survive. "The first major business combination arose before the Civil War in the railroad industry out of the need to join the growing East to the Western Frontier."[3] As more companies merged, more problems arose among businesses. Most of the problems dealt with stock in the companies. So in 1868 New Jersey enacted a statute that authorized corporations to hold capital stock of other corporations. As a result, the parent-subsidiary relationship was created among firms; it was subsequently adopted by most of the states.

By the beginning of the 1900s, this country was developing gigantic enterprises. In order to structure the formation of these enterprises, the Clayton Act was passed to control the development of monopolies. The number of mergers continued to increase rapidly throughout the 1950s. "In 1950 there were four acquisitions of listed companies in manufacturing and mining whose assets exceeded ten million dollars representing total assets of one hundred and seventy-three million dollars."[4] Because of the continuing increase of mergers and acquisitions, the Clayton Act was amended. "Section 7 of the Clayton Act provides that the act is violated where a corporation acquires assets or stock in another corporation and the effect of the acquisition may be substantially to lessen competition, or to tend to create monopoly."[5] The objective of this act is to maintain a competitive business economy.

During the 1960s, in addition to the traditional merger or acquisition involving two willing parties, a second type of acquisition gained popularity: the takeover. "In the takeover, a seller's management may oppose the acquisition or merger, but the buyer makes a direct bid to the seller's stockholders to acquire the seller's stock and thus control of the seller."[6] Initially most firms saw nothing wrong with the takeover procedure. It actually became an accepted and respectable method of acquisition in the mid-1960s. But toward the end of the 1960s the takeover bid was subjected to various degrees of threatened regulation. "The takeover bid came under attack for less obvious reasons, and resulted in the passage of the so called 'Williams Bill' to regulate cash tender offers."[7] This bill provides for the filing of specified information with SEC by any person intending to offer cash for publicly held stock.

The most recent discussions of business combinations have dealt with very large mergers (in terms of dollars) and many hostile takeovers. One of the current controversies is the Time–Paramount–Warner deal. It could end up as a hostile takeover if Paramount Communications Inc. wins the court case. "In court, the judge has to decide if Time Inc. put itself on the block on March 4, when it announced its original merger with Warner Communications Inc. If the judge decides that Time did put itself up for sale then the company may be forced to hold an auction in which Davis' [Paramount's CEO] bid, and others, would have to be considered."[8] If that is the case, Time would have to take the offer which benefits the shareholders the most.

From a management perspective, the shareholders feel as though they are being ignored. Michael F. Price, president of Heine Securities Corp., says, "I'm not happy with Time's management. It doesn't care about its shareholders."[9] During this episode it seems that Time did not allow its shareholders to vote on their deal. Shareholders feel that management is basically protecting itself in the Warner merger. And with the Paramount situation, Time's CEO is continuing to say they are not for sale. It could take up to a year before a decision is reached and until then there will be many doubts expressed by the companies, the management, and the shareholders.

EVALUATION

The game of mergers and acquisitions grew fast in the late 1960s, a time of great danger and high excitement in the financial canyons of the nation. Fortunes were pirated almost overnight, while respected companies went to the bottom and others fought desperately to survive. After the leading conglomerators carried the game too far, defensive tactics and strategies—spurred mostly by fear of takeovers and good business sense—caused the federal government to force the conglomerators to slow down. Congress began discussing restrictive legislation and a new Justice Department Antitrust Division Administration was created.

The federal decisions made the number of mergers and acquisitions drop sharply until the early 1970s, when takeover artists once again started to compile lists of potential victims. This time the game was not limited to superior conglomerators. Financially depressed companies realized that they could also play, provided they find target companies that suited their financial needs. So many new and fascinating things are happening on the financial front today that it may be our last frontier, where boldness and initiative are rewarded and the fainthearted or ir-resolute are crushed.

Mergers and acquisitions have become an integral part of big business, due to their money-making opportunities and means of letting com-panies stay competitive. The new wave of mergers and acquisitions started around 1982. According to Stephen C. Coley, a partner at McKinsey & Co., the future number of transactions will take a downturn, but it will not be a boom-or-bust cycle as was the 1960s and 1970s.[10]

In several studies, mergers of the 1960s and 1970s were given failing marks, because mergers of that era were paper-generated, unlike the economically generated mergers of today. This is one of the reasons that experts feel that the crash of the stock market on October 19, 1987 (Black Monday), had no adverse effects on the merger and acquisition game. According to IDD Information Services, nearly $162-billion worth of transactions were announced in the first few months of 1988, double the amount during the same period in 1987.[11] According to James Maher, head of mergers and acquisitions for First Boston Corporation, the num-ber of deals was high in the early months of 1988 due to low interest rates and a growing consensus that the economy had not been unduly influenced by the crash.[12]

In 1988 alone, billions of dollars were spent on mergers and acquisi-tions. According to Alfred Rappaport, a merger specialist at North-western University's graduate school of management, 1988 was the biggest year for mergers and takeovers.[13]

Merger and acquisition experts feel that the reason for this deals-down–values-up trend is the easy availability of credit and the intense competition for deals. Finances for taking a company private or for future transactions are readily available. Banks, investment firms, and LBO firms have access to pools of credit so immense that even the most audacious of schemes can be financed. Consider a few of the billion-dollar deals of 1988, such as Robert Campeau's extraordinary takeover of Federated Department Stores for $6.2 billion.

Although many buyouts and mergers have been successfully com-pleted, the black plague of the merger and acquisition game, restruc-turing, is incomplete. In the 1960s and 1970s one company bought another company and kept it. Today, companies are no longer simply bought to hold, but are broken up so that units can be resold for profit.

This buy up–break up trend has resulted in a clash of corporate cul-tures for many companies. This is one of the reasons many mergers fail. The struggle for control of acquired companies has also resulted in failed mergers, but due to outstanding restructuring methods most are suc-cessful. This is why experts urge that when looking for potential target companies one should look at its own corporate culture and try to acquire similar companies. When a company tries to combine different, and even opposite cultures, chaos is inevitable.

John Gardner, former U.S. Secretary of Health, Education and Welfare, points out that "chaos exacts an enormous toll on employees, in the form of anxiety, fear, and tension. That, in turn, leads to conscious and unconscious resistance to change, attempts at self-preservation, break downs in communication, a loss of commitment, and a powerful 'us-vs.-them' attitude. And when employees in the company being acquired behave this way, mergers will fail even if all the numbers indicate that they should succeed."[14]

A successful organization is one in which employees are productive, committed, self-generating, and creative. The merger of two companies with different corporate cultures seems to produce the opposite behavior pattern. The obvious way to avoid this type of corporate breakdown is for potential buyers to realize that the corporate culture has greater impact on a company's success than anything management can employ.

DO MERGERS REALLY WORK?

Not many mergers actually work. Most companies use a merger to diversify, which very often ends in failure. Mark Feldman of the Hay Group found that about one-third of all acquired companies are sold within five years, and that 90 percent of mergers never live up to the acquiring firm's expectations.[15]

One merger analyst, Morty Lefkoe, believes that the major reason for merger failure is the clash between corporate cultures. Corporate culture is the way an organization views itself, or its written and unwritten policies and procedures. One thing that can tear a merger apart is the attitude of "us versus them." This attitude, according to Lefkoe, ensures that the merger will not succeed. Lefkoe believes that if culture is the problem in a merger, the problem can never be solved. If employees want to come to work and are excited about their jobs, feeling that they make a difference in the company, there are lower costs, higher revenues, and greater customer satisfaction. If managers want to change the corporate culture, it must shake up the status quo so the employees are open to a new way of doing things.

REASONS FOR MERGERS

There are many reasons for corporate mergers in today's business world. Many managers feel that buying another company will give their own company better access to markets, products, technology, resources, and management talent. Buying a company may be less risky than building up a company through internal efforts. However, many studies show that deals between companies often do not live up to the acquirers' expectations. Several analysts feel that there are two ways to make acquisitions work. First, there must be a strategic fit between the acquirer and its target. Second, there is a need to match administrative systems, corporate cultures, or demographic characteristics.

There are inherent problems when a parent company analyzes a target. Top-level management may see a lack of organization or there may be too many people involved in the analysis. Top-level management may not be able to keep track of who is doing what, or how all their efforts will come together. This demonstrates how difficult the analytical process can be when a large group of specialists with a narrow focus is formed under time constraints. One item that is important, but often overlooked in the decision process, is operating considerations. Many line managers do not take part in presenting their views in the merger or acquisition analysis, and top-level managers believe that they have the skills needed to run a company after the acquisition has taken place.[16]

When managers are forced to close a deal quickly they may overlook strategic and organizational fit. Decision makers need secrecy when they are trying to concentrate on a merger decision. If the company learns of a merger, business as usual stops. The shareholders, employees, suppliers, customers, and competitors become uncertain of the stability of the company. A merger takes time, and if a manager can relate to a merger then he or she will be less willing to walk away from the decision process.

Mergers may take place for several reasons. The manager of an acquiring company may use the target company as a stepping stone for personal rewards or to enhance his own reputation. This may cause a company problems. Managers may want to close deals at any cost, whether beneficial to the acquiring company's future or not. Mergers are sometimes orchestrated to acquire new technologies. Mergers may be used in backward or forward integration. Backward integration is when a company merges to become closer to its raw materials. Forward integration occurs when a company merges to become closer to its customers. Growth in a company is another reason for merger. Managers must be careful if the only way for growth within the company is transfer to a newly acquired company. These managers may take valuable personnel from the base company with them.

PROBLEMS WITH MERGERS

It is beneficial to look at some failed mergers. In 1985, Mobil Corporation announced that it was going to drop Montgomery Ward and Co.

Mobil had bought Montgomery Ward in 1976 at a cost of $1.8 billion, and had invested $609 million in the company. Montgomery Ward had only produced $17 million net profit since the merger. What is an oil company doing in the clothing industry? This substantiates the fact that only like businesses should merge.

Some of the biggest failures have been in the mining industry.[17] When inflation and commodity prices were high, the mining industry controlled prices, raising them enormously. Now mining prices are lower, and mining companies are becoming burdens to their parent companies. Atlantic Richfield lost $785 million in 1984 when unloading Anaconda Mineral Co. Companies such as Gulf & Western, ITT, U.S. Industries, and Beatrice, once takeover kings, are now quickly dropping their target companies. Many companies keep pumping money into dying acquired firms. Is there a personal reason for this? Is there a reputation at stake?

McKinsey & Co.'s study of fifty-eight mergers undertaken between 1972 and 1983 asked two questions. Did the return on the total amount invested in the acquisitions exceed the cost of capital? Did they help the parent company outperform the competition in the stock market?[18] Results showed that twenty-eight of the fifty-eight mergers clearly failed both tests, and six others failed one. Again, the failed mergers were the mergers of unrelated businesses.

One mistake companies make is believing that skills in one business can be directly transferred to another. This was the mistake of the Philip Morris Company. Philip Morris thought that it could apply its cigarette business management skills to the 7UP Company and turn it into another Coca-Cola. What Philip Morris realized after seven years is what 7UP's top management already knew, that lemon-lime soft drinks have limited appeal compared to cola drinks.

SUCCESSFUL MERGERS

There are three phases in a successful merger, according to James T. Richman. In the first phase the acquiring firm makes a possible merger with another company known to the public. The second phase, which Richman calls the merger bargaining phase, is continued until the merger is complete. The third phase, which Richman terms the merger integration phase, is when the two companies combine.[19]

Richman notes that corporate officers taking part in mergers are duty-bound to their company. Sometimes self-interest of management is not in the best interest of the company. Corporate officers should relate their interests to benefit the company. There has to be a sense of corporate executive responsibility. Richman believes that corporate decision makers should be utilitarians, responding to the interests and concerns of their stockholders, employees, and consumers.[20]

According to Allen Michel and Israel Shaked, there must be "synergy" before a merger can be justified. In order to obtain synergy, a firm's profits with the target firm must be greater than the profits of the original company.[21] Michel and Shaked found that the number of pure conglomerate mergers had grown from 14.9 percent in the 1950s to 36.4 percent in the 1970s, and the number of vertical and horizontal integration mergers had dropped from 43.7 percent in the 1950s to 24.5 percent in the 1970s.[22] Michel and Shaked feel that synergy is revealed by the rate of return to the stockholders. Thus, the price of the shares should be raised, even if profits do not increase until a much later date. However, a study by Robert Langetieg points out that acquiring firms' shares began to fall seven months before a merger, and continued to drop after the merger. This suggests that a stockholder with a well-diversified portfolio should not expect the target company to boost yields above the premerger yield.[23]

CONTEMPORARY MERGERS

By examining various industries one can see that mergers are beginning to change. The past ten to fifteen years show a down trend from high-volume mass production toward more specialized customized production.[24] The steel industry has been following this strategy. For example, LTV's J&L Steel merged with Republic Steel. When they decided to merge, the agreement was to combine their most successful product lines and drop the rest. They are shipping fewer tons and fewer products, but what they are shipping is of better quality.

The auto industry is using mergers to enhance existing business and to create new business. In 1985 General Motors obtained Hughes Aircraft. Hughes Aircraft is one of the largest defense electronics companies; General Motors can use that technology to contribute to its car-making skills.

Another fact that has created more mergers is deregulation. There were many consolidations among airlines, railroads, and trucking companies due to deregulation. Mergers had banks owning other banks across state lines. In 1984 there were 232 bank mergers, and experts believe that by 1990 banks will decrease in number from 15,000 to less than 10,000.[25] The reason for large mergers in the food industry is economies of scale. Harris Upham states that "the fastest and cheapest way to serve various areas of the grocery-store shelf is to acquire them."[26]

The recent burst of takeover mania involving food and brand-name consumer products is reminiscent of the oil company merger craze of the early 1980s. Buyers see value in these companies, with their potential for economies of scale in global production, marketing, and distribution.

They see nothing wrong with the astounding prices, such as the $25-billion bid by Kohlberg, Kravis, & Roberts for RJR Nabisco. Do these brand-name takeovers make sense and will they work, or will they fail spectacularly if the debt-ridden buyers suddenly find themselves facing an economic recession?

When merging with another company, the acquiring firm must take a look at the human side of the merger. Many acquirers look over the target, applying their own management methods, and put their own people in the target company. The target company may become so bureaucratic that the management in place loses interest. This was the case with Avon's acquisition in 1979 of Tiffany & Co., a New York jeweler.

Avon bought $94 million of Tiffany's stock, believing that they could automate Tiffany's billing department and modernize their stores. Avon invested $53 million in Tiffany over five years. Sales increased but profits dropped. In 1984, Tiffany had sales of $135 million, but lost $5 million in profits. So in 1984, Avon sold the company to William Chaney for about the same price it had paid for it. After Avon purchased Tiffany, Tiffany started to sell jewelry of lesser quality and price. Before Avon purchased Tiffany, they concentrated sales on the wealthy. This group consisted of about five thousand people. Avon allowed Tiffany's expenses to grow. Chaney got rid of much of its inventory and cut the staff by 10 percent. By running a leaner company, Chaney increased profits by $11 million in the first year.[27] This indicates that a large company can run a smaller company into the ground. Many large companies are trying to relate their management style to an acquired company, and it is not working.

LEGISLATION

State laws, soon to be followed by federal laws, are being implemented to limit takeover activity. The March 1988 Supreme Court securities laws decision is designed to protect target companies.[28] However, these laws have been largely ineffective, and some argue that the laws only benefit existing management. "Merger mania" is continuing to grow, as corporations make use of clever loopholes. One tactic used by corporate buyers is to set up "mirror" subsidiaries of an acquired company and sell the stocks instead of the assets. However, the government does fight corporate raiders. In December 1987, Congress passed reforms that require the regular 34 percent corporate tax on gains of $15 million.[29]

It appears that corporate raiders cannot be stopped because they buy and shed assets so quickly. But, according to Robert Willard, head of mergers and acquisitions at Prudential-Bache Securities Inc., these raiders are slapped with taxes on gains, forcing them to bid less than those who buy to hold and incur no tax.[30] If all the cash-rich corporations with the interest and ability to buy and hold do so, it will spell even more trouble for corporate raiders. They would have to play the game without tax breaks and mirrors—in short, by the rules. Although mergers, buyouts, and acquisitions often cloud the true state of the economy, there is no need for additional rules and restrictions against these intercorporate deals, which are more healthful than harmful to the nation's business according to David Pauly.[31]

President Reagan facilitated mergers in the 1980s by offering a tax reduction program that was passed with bipartisan support in 1981. This tax reduction program helped General Electric purchase RCA. GE paid $6.28 billion in cash for the ninth largest corporation in the *Fortune* 500.[32] GE paid $185 million in taxes, but over four years it reported profits of $9.5 billion. Therefore, over four years its tax rate was only one percent. Large corporations have used their tax breaks to buy other large corporations. In such a sale consumers and employees are not taken into consideration. Research has shown that large corporations grow weaker with size. Many executives "loot" the rich sections of their corporation and do not pay any attention to the poor ones. The people who get hurt in such mergers are employees and customers. Workers have to deal with plant closings, capital fights, union busting, and sudden divestitures. Consumers have less leverage to affect quality and price decisions. The only winners are the men at the top of each corporation and the lawyers and brokers who help make the deals.

EFFECTS ON EMPLOYEES

Mergers do not affect employees. A study by Robert Hayes found that only 42 percent of the top managers remained with an acquired firm for as long as five years.[33] However, he found that those managers who stayed took time to investigate the buying company. Mitchell L. Marks believes that communication in a corporation is very important. Employees who are not kept informed about a merger become suspicious. Studies show that if employees take an active part in merger planning, it gives them a sense of commitment. The acquiring company can gain valuable information from the employees of the acquired organization.[34]

British consultants note that the increase in the size of a company after a merger can cause stress. This may lead to bureaucratization and impersonality influencing employee motivation. It may also hinder decision making. Two major stressors associated with mergers are uncertainty and insecurity. When a merger is announced, it may raise fear and anxieties in employees. Employees wonder how the merger will change their work situation, and they may feel a loss of control. Mergers are perceived as a "threat to one's equilibrium, accustomed relationships, norms, statuses, and work behaviors."[35] It has been noted that executives in acquired firms were more stressed, anxious, and pessimistic than were the executives in acquiring firms.

Employees are aware of how a merger can affect their careers, rewards, and daily activities, and are afraid of being terminated, transferred, or having new bosses. A study by Timothy Costello suggests that older employees feel more secure in their jobs than younger employees. Furthermore, not all mergers are bad. Mergers may increase compensation and produce attractive job reassignments. Some small firms may lose their identity when they merge with a large firm. Employees may find it harder to be loyal to the new organization. Of all the people affected by a merger, the chief executive officer is probably affected the most. A CEO's entrepreneurial motivation is often reduced by an acquisition. With the loss of autonomy and top status, many CEOs resign.

Mergers are time-consuming and stressful, and require top management's full attention. The most successful mergers are mergers between related corporations. Corporations must also take into consideration the employee. Employees can be very helpful during the time of a merger.

In 1984 there were 2,543 mergers with a dollar value of $122 billion. Successful mergers are mergers that deal with related businesses. A merger is also more likely to succeed if the management of the acquired company stays in top management. According to W. T. Grimm & Co., from 1980 to 1985 the number of divestitures had jumped 36 percent with a dollar value of $29.4 billion.[36]

THE IMPACT OF MERGERS

The effects of mergers on the workforce extend beyond those who suddenly find themselves unemployed. As we have already pointed out, fear created among executives may encourage them to secure excess compensation, resulting in cynicism. Morale can suffer if companies, subsidiaries, and employees are shifted around; staff reductions will create stiffer competition for mangerial jobs.

The implications of the merger craze for society are even more disturbing:

1. It may induce government regulation of the economy, especially in the event of a recession.
2. It gives top executives a disproportionate effect on the economy, making the economy more vulnerable to bad decisions when there are few executives.
3. It allows a foreign company that is purchasing a U.S. industry the ability to

acquire more of it. This encourages protectionism, which has a negative effect on the economy.

For all the dangers, the surge in mergers may do some good. Many companies, forced to reduce debt rapidly, cut frills and become more efficient. As companies concentrate their efforts on fewer businesses, the economy may benefit.

THE FUTURE OF MERGERS AND ACQUISITIONS IN THE UNITED STATES

The year 1988 was a record year for mergers. More mergers were announced in the first six months of 1988 than all of 1985; the value of these takeovers topped that for all of 1984.

Looming as a potential roadblock to more merger activity are takeover prices as high as Wall Street has seen in years. A new obstacle for raiders—and for all suitors—is the growing arsenal of defense weapons open to target companies. The proliferation of state antitakeover laws, coupled with repeated court victories for poison pill defenses, has strengthened the hands of companies fighting hostile takeovers.

Corporate buyers, heartened by the favorable outlook on the economy and interest rates, should stay busy, as individual raiders are hurt by judicial and legislative antitakeover moves. Experts predict that cash tender offers are still the best bet to overcome toughened takeover defenses, and will become increasingly popular. Foreign investment in U.S. firms will remain keen; for the first time in years, U.S. suitors are seeking European targets, due to the upcoming 1992 Common Market consolidation.[37]

THE FUTURE OF MERGERS IN EUROPE

The European Economic Community (EEC) is fast approaching the 1992 single market, and is now locked in debate over a common policy for mergers and acquisitions. A breakup in August 1988 of a joint bid for whiskey maker Irish Distillers demonstrated both Brussels' growing power to intervene in takeovers and the need for a clear policy.

Without firm rules, there is likely to be chaos; as things stand now, a company's freedom to maneuver is very uneven across EEC. Some countries, such as Denmark, Italy, and Belgium, have few or no laws governing mergers. Dutch and German legislation, on the other hand, forms highly protectionist shields against foreign purchasers. Great Britain has the most liberal operating environment but lays down strict rules about bidding and stock disclosure. Portugal is still deciding what kind of merger policy it wants.

Cross-border mergers are on the rise as European companies brace themselves for the intense competition of a borderless, unified Internal Market, EEC's 1992 goal. According to the latest report on competition activity, 708 mergers, minority acquisitions, and joint ventures took place in 1987 among the community's one thousand largest firms, up 27 percent from 1986.

The major obstacle to forging a common policy is political; no matter how it is worded, no version will please all twelve governments. No new merger regulation will have an answer to all situations; and the wording is less important than its ongoing interpretation before the courts.[38]

INTERNATIONAL MERGERS

Foreign investment in U.S. companies is increasing. Though the Japanese are not exactly roaring into the U.S. mainstream of corporate success with its purchases of CBS Records, Firestone Tire and Rubber, and Sony Corporation, these acquisitions cannot be ignored. Japanese buyers have been educating themselves in U.S. deal making. "There was a stereotypical view of Japanese buyers as very plodding and very cautious," says Merrill Lynch's Jeffery Berenson.[39] Berenson believes that the Japanese "have become much more tuned in to the way the merger and acquisitions practice exists here and are much more aggressive, much quicker, much more transactions-oriented and much more decisive in their approach to buying U.S. properties."[40]

Other countries getting into the game are France, Germany, and Italy. France's recent deals in the United States include Hachette's $465-million purchase of Grolier. The Italians have been especially visible in the U.S. health care field. As for the Germans, their interest in the United States varies from one business to another. Other countries to watch are Spain and Korea.

It should be pointed out that the flow of money is not going both ways; Americans are not rushing overseas to buy up foreign companies. In the opinion of Stephen Blum, co-director of mergers and acquisitions for Peat Marwick, "some legislative restrictions to foreign takeovers are more than likely, in the near future."[41]

All this asset swapping is creating a more rational competitive system of business today. No one is saying that mergers and takeovers can keep up the current pace forever. However, if the current acquisitions patterns continue, more takeovers will succeed and there will be better competitors in the United States and in the world.

NOTES

1. Charles A. Scharf, *Acquisitions, Mergers, Sales, and Takeovers: A Handbook with Forms* (Englewood Cliffs, N.J.: Prentice-Hall, 1971), p. 3.

2. Thomas Boyd and S. Winton Korn, *Accounting for Management Planning and Decision Making* (New York: Wiley, 1969), p. 221.

3. Isay Stemp, *Corporate Growth Strategies* (American Management Association, New York, N.Y., 1970), p. 399.

4. Ibid., p. 401.

5. Scharf, *Acquisitions, Mergers, Sales, and Takeovers*, p. 120.

6. Ibid., p. 1.

7. Ibid., p. 2.

8. "Time's Counterattack Is Drawing Acid Reviews," *Business Week* (July 3, 1989): 26.

9. Ibid.

10. Judith Dobrzynski, "A New Strain of Merger Mania," *Business Weekly* (March 21, 1988): 124.

11. Michael Dunn, "Corporate Finance," *Barron's* (February 24, 1988): 39.

12. Randy Scott, "Mergers & Acquisitions," *Forbes* (June 2, 1988): 59.

13. Dobrzynski, "New Strain of Merger Mania," p. 125.

14. Morty Lefkoe, "Why So Many Mergers Fail," *Fortune* (July 20, 1987): 116.

15. Wayne E. Green, "Confusion over Merger-Disclosure Law," *Wall Street Journal* (June 24, 1988).

16. David B. Jemison and Sim B. Sitkin, "Acquisitions—The Process Can Be a Problem," *Harvard Business Review* (March–April 1986): 109.

17. John Adams, "Do Mergers Really Work?" *Business Week* (June 3, 1985): 88.

18. Ibid., p. 89.

19. James D. Richman, "Merger Decision Making: An Ethical Analysis and Recommendation," *California Management Review* (Fall 1984): 177.

20. Ibid., p. 181.

21. Allen Michel and Israel Shaked, "Evaluating Merger Performance," *California Management Review* (Spring 1985): 109.

22. Ibid.

23. Ibid., p. 116.

24. Monroe W. Karmin, "Mergers Give U.S. Industry Tougher Skin," *U.S. News and World Report* (July 8, 1985): 47.

25. Ibid., p. 48.

26. Ibid.

27. Claire Poole and Jeffrey A. Trachtenberg, "Bear Hug," *Forbes* (November 16, 1987): 187.

28. Green, "Confusion over Merger-Disclosure Law."

29. Catherine Yong, "The New Tax Angle in the Merger Game," *Business Week* (March 21, 1988): 138.

30. Ann Brown, "Merger Ethics," *Forbes* (November 4, 1985): 25.

31. David Pauly, "Merger Inc.," *Newsweek* (December 9, 1985): 47.

32. Michael Madding, "Big Is Not Better," *Nation* (December 28, 1985): 699.

33. Mitchell Lee Marks, "Merging Human Resources," *Merger and Acquisition Magazine* (Summer 1982): 39.

34. Ibid., p. 40.

35. Ibid., p. 41.

36. Adams, "Do Mergers Really Work?" p. 88.

37. Brian Burrough, "Takeover Boom Is Expected to Continue after a Strong First Half," *Wall Street Journal* (July 5, 1988).

38. Brooks Tigner, "Brussels Drafting One-Stop Shopping Rules for Growing Wave of European Takeovers," *International Management* (October 1988).

39. Lefkoe, "Why So Many Mergers Fail," p. 120.

40. Robert Grimm, "Mergers," *Forbes* (September 12, 1984): 68.

41. Ibid., p. 106.

BIBLIOGRAPHY

Berry, John. "Any Deal Is Double." *Mergers & Acquisitions* (June 1988): 56.

Committee of Experts on Restrictive Business Practices. *Mergers and Competition Policy*. Paris: Organization for Economic Co-Operation and Development, 1974.

Karp, Irwin. "Let's Look Much Harder at Mergers." *Publishers Weekly* (April 17, 1987): 18.

Sauerhaft, Stan. "The Mergers of Today." *Business Weekly* (October 12, 1984): 351.

4

CORPORATE TAKEOVERS

The term *takeover* refers to a situation in which an outside force gathers enough money to buy a controlling amount of stock in a company. The outside force thus takes over the target company. With the increased threat of takeovers, corporations have been forced to reshape their operating procedures and structures. Today almost any corporation might become the target of a takeover. Business and management must be aware of the characteristics that make firms likely takeover targets, and defenses they can use to protect their companies.

TAKOVER ACTIVITY

Business transactions have been recorded since ancient times with the bartering of goods. Following the Industrial Revolution, transactions have become increasingly complex. Takeover activity seems to stem from the U.S. deregulation of the 1970s. Most major industries were affected at this time, including the airline, trucking, railroad, gas and oil, telecommunications and broadcasting industries. This deregulation led to a period of corporate mergers. Companies would merge in an attempt to dominate the market. Some significant mergers that occurred at this time were Chevron, Gulf Oil, Mobil, and Superior Oil.[1] A study in 1976 showed that there were 1,100 mergers and acquisitions of companies with assets of one million dollars or greater in the United States. A 1985 study showed that number had climbed to over 3,000.[2]

Merger activity has evolved into takeover activity. Takeovers are relatively new and the past five years show an increasingly favorable environment for corporate takeovers. For many reasons, takeovers became more widespread in the 1980s. One major reason became apparent in the stock market crash of October 1987.[3] This crash left enormous capital to be used by corporations, raiders, and investment banks. This excess capital made it favorable to take over a company even if the odds seemed high. Also, more corporations and individuals began to compete for market dominance due to the current economic cycle.[4]

Most of the companies that have been taken over have tried to prevent it. The term *hostile takeover* is used to describe this situation. The frequency of hostile takeovers is frightening. In the past two years nearly 240 American companies valued at over $100 million have been the targets of hostile takeover attempts.[5]

The instigators of hostile takeovers are often wealthy and influential individuals. Some of the more successful individuals involved in takeovers are referred to as corporate raiders. Currently, people such as Brian Beazer, Irwin Jacobs, and Sir James Goldsmith are successful corporate raiders.

Corporations, due to factors such as the weakening of the junk bond market and the widely fluctuating stock market, have become involved in takeovers.

CHARACTERISTICS OF TAKEOVER TARGETS

A survey conducted by *Fortune* magazine revealed the characteristics that make a company a likely takeover target. *Fortune* asked buyout specialists, money managers, and arbitrageurs how they spot potential targets. Most importantly, they look for companies with a strong, steady cash flow. Analysts are extremely interested in companies with earnings after interest payments, taxes, dividends, and capital expenditures. Another attraction is recession-resistant companies that boast valuable brand-names. Borden, for example, can use product names such as Wise Potato Chips, Cracker Jacks, and Elmer's Glue.[6] *Fortune*'s study also suggests that potential targets have little long-term debt, under 50 percent capitalization. This can be determined by dividing the amount of cash on a company's balance sheet by the number of shares outstanding and comparing that figure with the stock price. Any stock selling for less than three times its cash per share looks especially good. A final characteristic is stocks whose trading volume has spurted. This can tip off an interested buyer.

THE TAKEOVER BID

If one company or individual decides to acquire another company, it puts in a takeover bid. A takeover bid is an "offer to buy securities of a corporation made directly to the shareholders of the corporation for the purpose of gaining control of the corporation."[7] The offer may be for either cash or securities of the offerer, and it may be made with or without the approval of management of the target company. There are two types of takeover bids: a tender offer and a registered exchange offer.

A tender offer is when the offer to buy the stock is made for cash. The tender offer has long been available as a means of gaining control of a corporation. The tender offer is subject to regulation by SEC, however. When making a tender offer, the corporation must file with SEC if the corporation becomes owner of more than 5 percent of securities. Laws also require that the offer remain effective for at least ten days. This gives substance to the requirement that the offerer acquire shares on a pro rata basis where an excess of the number of shares sought to be purchased are tendered in the first ten days after the tender offer is given.[8] In addition, the New York Stock Exchange has established a policy requiring that all shareholders of a company be given an opportunity to participate on equal terms in any tender offer.

The registered exchange offer is when an offer to buy stock is made for securities, usually to the public. A problem arises with the maintenance of secrecy. The offerer will wish to achieve as much surprise as possible, in order to allow management of the target company as little time as possible to take defensive action. The management of the offerer must decide whether it wishes to acquire stock of the target company in the open market. A prior acquisition of stock gives an offerer a head start. However, the prior acquisition of securities of the target company may lead to information leaks, which may affect an increase in the cost of the offer, thus alerting a watchful management that a takeover bid is coming.[9]

ADVANTAGES AND DISADVANTAGES

Takeovers have both advantages and disadvantages. Any advantages will usually be gained by stockholders, because the value of the company's target stock is usually driven up by the takeover. Advocates of takeovers also cite an average posttakeover value increase of 8.4 percent.[10] Disadvantages that can result are the loss of jobs, employees, and subsidiaries; the loss of a company's morale and stability; the debt that a raider often leaves the company; and the debt incurred resisting the takeover, which can run into millions of dollars. One more disadvantage is the neglect of a company's long-term goals. Most corporations today attempt to be socially responsible, spending large amounts of money on environmental issues and concerns, safety programs, and community projects. Once a corporation is taken over, these social projects are jeopardized.

REASONS FOR TAKEOVERS

There are many reasons for the large number of takeovers today, the foremost being that hostile takeovers are relatively simple ventures. A substantial portion of the stock will be in the hands of arbitrageurs before the company being taken over is prepared to defend itself.

Another reason for the large number of takeover attempts is the diversification of the 1960s and 1970s. The diversified structure facilitates the liquidation of subsidiary companies for profit. The money gained from the liquidations is then used to pay off the debts incurred in the takeover process.

Finally, almost all takeovers and attempted takeovers have resulted in a large profit to the initiator of the takeover, whether the takeover succeeded or not. This may seem unusual, but when the process of a takeover is examined the reason becomes quite clear. Often a takeover begins with the purchase of a large amount of the target company's stock, which causes the price of the stock to rise. If a takeover fails, the raider can sell the stock he has acquired at a higher price. Gains from this type of activity can be sizable, as was the case when Sir James Goldsmith failed to take over the Goodyear Tire Company. Goodyear repurchased its stock from Goldsmith, and he made a profit of $90 million.[11]

Combinations of the above factors have led to an increase in takeover activity. The common factor seems to be quick profit.

FINANCING TAKEOVERS

The amount of money needed to accomplish a takeover can be billions of dollars in many cases. Investors must find ways to finance takeover attempts. The most obvious method is to obtain the lowest possible acquisition price. The importance of the acquisition price is emphasized by John Coyne, who suggests that no more important decision will be made in the course of a buyout, and that "the implications of that decision will have a fundamental bearing on the health of the businees after the buyout and, indeed may well be the key factor in determining whether or not it survives."[12]

Another method is to obtain a loan from a bank. Takeover initiators explain what they are going to do and how they plan to do it. After the bank is convinced the plan will be profitable, the money is granted. More often than not, the bank lends the money requested because, as stated previously, even if the takeover fails a profit can be made from the reselling of the purchased stock. Financial support can also be gained through the issuance of junk bonds, which are not rated by investment services and often pay 3 percent more than less risky securities. The attractiveness of junk bonds provides an enormous amount of money.

Other sources of financial support are investment firms and other investors. An example of this is the investment company of Shearson, Lehman Brothers and fellow raider T. Boone Pickens, Jr., who loaned $355 million and $150 million, respectively, to help raider Paul Bilzerian acquire enough money to take over the Singer Company. Incidentally, the company had to be dismantled to repay the loans.[13]

RESISTING TAKEOVERS

There are many ways a company can resist a takeover attempt. One defensive measure involves making the company look unattractive to the corporate raider. Management can leverage the firm by restructuring it through the sale or liquidation of assets by creating "poison pills." (This is when stockholders authorize new securities to be issued in the event of a hostile takeover, in order to raise the cost.)

Another form of defense is the "white knight lockup agreement." Here, management of the target company grants a friendly third party the option to purchase enough stock to gain control of the target company. An example of this was when Marathon Oil Company merged with U.S. Steel, and avoided being acquired by Mobil.[14] Another typical defense used by management is the "Pac Man" defense. This is when a counter-tender offer is made for the stock of the would-be acquirer.

A very powerful method is restructuring the company. A common restructuring method is buying back the company's own stock and going private. The most successful way to reacquire stock is through a leveraged buyout. When a public company becomes a private one, the CEO takes direct responsibility for something he actually owns.[15] The buying back of stock often increases the debts of the company and further decreases the likelihood of takeover. Another kind of restructuring is the divesting of unprofitable companies. This eliminates the possibility of a takeover initiator obtaining profit by divesting divisions.

A powerful defensive measure is making a company unaffordable.

This can be accomplished in a number of ways, such as offering specialized low-priced stock purchasing plans to stockholders if a takeover percentage reaches a "trigger percentage" of the total. Outstanding stock often deters a potential takeover.[16] Providing compensation insurance to upper management makes a company less affordable. According to Thomas Murray, nearly half of the largest five hundred American firms pack golden parachutes to break the financial fall of top executives. Recently, ousted chairman Sam Armacost received a $1.7-million package from the Bank America Corporation as a golden parachute settlement.[17]

Another method of resisting takeovers is a plea for friendly takeover by other firms, which assures jobs for the future and deters "Pac Man" ploys.

LEGAL DEVELOPMENTS

Twenty-seven states have passed laws limiting shareholder rights, thus enhancing management's ability to resist takeovers. Minnesota, Indiana, and most notably, Delaware have passed legislation restricting corporate raiders. More than a dozen states have followed in enacting takeover laws. Corporations located in states lacking takeover legislation have threatened to move if laws are not enacted to protect them. Delaware, the home of half of the companies listed on the New York Stock Exchange, has been the center of a heated controversy.[18] A recent bill enacted by the State of Delaware, seen as too favorable to management, was immediately challenged in the courts by the Campeau and the Black and Decker Corporations, both of which were attempting takeovers of other Delaware corporations.

Unless the federal government intervenes, state governments will continue to address the takeover issue. A sound basis for government intervention is the many state laws which necessitate unconstitutional interference with interstate commerce.[19]

TAKEOVER PROBLEMS

The hostile takeover of a company is a traumatic experience at all levels of the target company. Concern and worry greatly affect morale and stability. *INC* magazine provides an example of this situation: "Wall Street guys come in and load up all the debt. That created nothing but headaches for the guys doing the work. You don't have any stability on the staff. There's chaos at the top, and it runs through everything a company does."[20] A takeover often results in loss of jobs, employees, and subsidiaries. Many stakeholders (suppliers, buyers, and communities) are also interested in the action.

Another problem associated with takeovers is massive debt. This debt, coupled with the debt incurred by the company while trying to prevent the takeover, eventually weakens the firm.

Also, many regard financial support as an omen. Even though dividend payments are not a factor of the revenue, interest paid on the loans is. In fact, some companies can be so burdened that their main revenue objective is to pay interest payments rather than the actual debt. Furthermore, some believe that inappropriate buyouts are being financed and therefore straining the funds from useful investments. Generally, the debt incurred from buyout deals can only be managed by those companies able to economize, increase revenues, and increase profits relative to interest and debt payments.

Finally, a major problem with takeovers is the resultant neglect of long-term social goals. Many corporations presently spend millions of dollars on environmental concerns, safety programs, and community projects. When money once used for these projects is redirected toward takeover activities, it is unlikely that those projects will receive any funding. Robert Mercer, chairman and CEO of the Goodyear Tire and Rubber Company, states that "a raider's idea of a clean environment is that, after swapping paper back and forth in a frenzy, you sell out at the last minute and stash the money in a Swiss bank account." This perversion of financial power has no redeeming social value, and will not create any real wealth.[21]

BENEFITS OF TAKEOVERS

Aside from the problems discussed above, takeovers do provide some benefits. One benefit is the effect on stockholders. Stockholders benefit from a takeover attempt because these activities drive up the value of the company's stock. Many studies have reported gains between 16 percent and 34 percent in takeover situations. During 1984 and 1985 alone, takeovers generated $75 billion in premiums for shareholders. Another benefit cited by advocates of takeovers is an 8.4 percent average increase in the value of a business after a takeover, as documented in a study for the Twentieth Century Fund.[22] This, however, reflects only short-term gain and sheds little light on the company's eventual worth.

Another benefit is that financial institutions provide tremendous funding. The management buyer has the assets and the reputation of the company as collateral. However, as valuable investments for banks, the earnings of a buyout are also reasons for investing. Buyouts are very attractive because of the front-end fees. Usually, in order for a buyout to commence, banks require a significant "service charge" for their enormous loan. Furthermore, banks are attracted by the interest rates. Since buyouts are encouraged by the government, financial institutions are able to charge an interest rate four or five points above the prime interest rate.[23] Many regard financial support as beneficial to both the economy and the particular company. First, the capital provided aids in the restructuring of a company so it can be more efficient. Furthermore, some believe that with the added funds, introduction and development of product lines will be significantly improved. Finally, the company will become future-oriented, increasing its value and enabling its debts to be paid.

Perhaps the most beneficial aspect of the leveraged buyout is charging off large mortgage interest payments. Operating profits not covered by depreciation allowances will be largely offset by huge interest payments. In the early years of a buyout many companies pay little or no corporate tax.

Another substantial advantage to going private is the ability to turn the company around and go public again. Some buyout deals are paid off in time, and companies are legitimately owned. Most often, however, more debt is assumed to make acquisitions and many bought-out companies go public again, scoring a second success in the new issues market.

A benefit to management is its ability to "own" its own company without direction from any elected board of directors. Management can, under the stricter parameters of the debt service, back out of unnecessary operations and be forced into running "lean and mean." Without shareholders looking at quarterly profit statements, managers can focus on long-term profit goals more compatible with their new financial liabilities. With more personal stakes, management will truly have to keep alert and hone their business skills.

Finally, benefits include increased career opportunities, increased security of supply, and increased economic opportunites in the surrounding community.[24]

THE ROLE OF MANAGEMENT

As previously discussed, during a hostile takeover management must become aware and practice the defensive strategies they have developed. Management, along with the board of directors, can defeat a hostile takeover if the situation is not ignored. Management has the power and ability to defeat the takeover attempt.

THE ROLE OF THE BOARD OF DIRECTORS

The board of directors is composed of inside and outside members. Their main objective is to hire, fire, and compensate top-level decision managers and to ratify and monitor important decisions. Like management, the board is critical to the running and structure of the corporation. The board is just as responsible as management in defending the corporation in a takeover attempt. There have been two principles applied by the courts in dealing with the responsibilities that boards have in the event of a takeover: "When the board's decision has taken on the appropriate defensive tactic, it must be reasonable in relation to the perceived threat to the corporation."[25] It is assumed that the board will always act in the best interest of the corporation. Another principle is that once the board takes action toward selling the company or approving a change of control of the company, its duty changes. The initial duty for the best interest of its shareholders has changed. Its main focus becomes treating all bidders fairly and maximizing prices.

THE ROLE OF CORPORATE RAIDERS

Most hostile takeovers are conducted by corporate raiders. These are the people with big business know-how. Once they hit big, they go on to become financial sharks. These are individuals with influence, financial capacity, and corporate savy who can threaten and take over a company. Corporate raiders take over companies for several reasons. This type of person is not afraid to phase out unproductive divisions, restructure companies, and liquidate assets of the companies acquired.[26] Corporate raiders want to make companies productive. Another reason for takeover attempts is liquidation of subsidiary companies for profit.

Most takeovers result in sizable profits to the corporate raider, whether or not they succeed. One big-name raider known for his large takeovers is Asher Edelman. His net worth is currently estimated at $100 million. Some of his bigger deals have been Burlington Industries (1987), in which he made a $65-million profit, and Ponderosa (1987), which was a $300-million investment. The Belzberg Brothers have also made a name for themselves, currently valued at $300 million. Some of their bigger deals include Scovill (1985), in which they made a $540-million investment and Gulf (1984), in which they made a $70-million profit. But perhaps the biggest name on Wall Street today is Sir James Goldsmith. He is currently valued at $1 billion. His biggest deals include Goodyear (1987), in which he made a $90-million profit, Crown Zellerback (1985), a $50-

million investment, and Diamond International (1980), in which a $500-million profit was made.[27]

RECENT TAKEOVER BIDS

In 1986, Sealy, Inc., was taken over by the Ohio Mattress Company. Sealy, opposing the takeover, tried to buy out the firm using a leveraged buyout. However, the stockholders became suddenly incommunicado and Sealy lost the fight. This exemplifies a hostile takeover in which management and the board of directors did not neglect the buyout.

The years 1988 and 1989 were record-breaking years for business transactions. Takeovers, acquisitions, restructurings, public offerings, and stock buyouts on *Fortune*'s annual list of the largest deals added up to $111.8 billion. Deal makers took in $68.7 million in advising fees. The number one transaction of the year was Philip Morris's unsolicited bid for Kraft, which was at first rejected but later accepted when the price was raised. The company was purchased for $12.9 billion. The management and board of directors seemed to be in favor of this particular takeover.[28]

Another major takeover was the hostile bid by Hoffmann-La Roche, a Swiss pharmaceutical giant, for Sterling Drug. However, Hoffmann lost and Eastman Kodak then took over Sterling Drug. Management and the board of directors of Sterling Drug were not in favor of this takeover.

SCM Corporation, a chemical and manufacturing company, was taken over by Hanson Trust. When the bid was offered, SCM tried a leveraged buyout. However, the tender offer never went as high as Hanson's, so SCM lost its battle to save the firm. Management and the board of directors were not in favor of this takeover.

Other recent takeovers are Maxwell Communication's acquisition of Macmillan Publishing. GE's acquisition of Borg-Warner, Sony's acquisition of CBS Records, and Dun and Bradstreet's acquisition of MIS International.[29]

RESOLUTIONS

With the continued upsurge of corporate takeovers, more legal restraints are being placed on corporations and corporate raiders. This section deals with the government's role in corporate takeovers. The government is acting on behalf of business, stepping in to protect businesses from being taken over.

The Federal Reserve Board has recently moved to restrict the ability of corporate raiders to finance acquisitions through the sale of junk bonds. This new law will reduce raiders' ability to obtain financing. The 1986 tax law contains provisions that may reduce the attractiveness of takeover targets. One law states that a target corporation's assets will be considered sold for a fair market value at the time of the merger, with taxes immediately due on the appreciated value of the assets.[30] Another provision prohibits deductions for greenmail payments. Further, a 1989 Supreme Court decision enacted several state laws aimed at protecting local companies from hostile takeovers.

The most important deterrent of hostile takeovers is SEC's successful prosecutions for insider trading of leading Wall Street actors such as arbitrageurs, corporate raiders, and other persons specializing in defending management against takeover threats. SEC's biggest scandal was the indictment of the risk arbitrageur Ivan Boesky. Boesky bought up target stocks on tips in hopes of backing a successful takeover. By buying up the stock, he would help the raider by increasing the price of the stock.

THE FUTURE OF THE COMPANY AND SOCIETY

With new laws being passed and old laws being enforced, we will begin to see a halt in hostile takeovers. Companies are following stricter regulations which will discourage certain destructive practices. Takeovers that are welcome and friendly are respected by society, while hostile takeovers are viewed as a hindrance to the economy. Hostile takeovers serve only to disrupt the life of a corporation.[31] Scandals that inform society of the misconduct of business usurp the glory of the corporate raider. Also, a takeover distorts financial priorities, resulting in a halt of social programs. Society wants to see the corporation act to better the economy and society. When the corporation becomes disorganized and disrupted, people become concerned and view this disruption negatively.

With an increased knowledge of corporate takeovers and with government regulations, the hostile takeover will eventually be controlled. The number will begin to decrease in the upcoming new wave of business. Takeovers will still exist, but will be increasingly friendly.

NOTES

1. Carol J. Billingham, "Hostile Corporate Takeovers: Why and How Their Numbers Grow," *Mid-American Journal of Business* (March 1987): 4–8.
2. Dwight Harshbarger, "Takeovers: A Tale of Loss, Change, and Growth," *Executive* (November 1987): 339–43.
3. Ibid.

4. Resa King, "Takeovers Are Back but Now the Frenzy Is Gone," *Business Week* (February 1989): 24–25.

5. Robert Mercer, "Raiders Might Be after Your Company Next," *Industry Week* (June 29, 1987): 14.

6. Thomas Moore, "How the 12 Top Raiders Rate," *Fortune* (September 28, 1987): 44–54.

7. Charles A. Scharf, *Acquisitions, Mergers, Sales, and Takeovers: A Handbook with Forms* (Englewood Cliffs, N.J.: Prentice-Hall, 1971), 159.

8. Ibid., p. 163.

9. Ibid.

10. Abbass F. Alkhafaji, *A Stakeholder Approach to Corporate Governance: Managing in a Dynamic Environment* (New York: Quorum, 1989), pp. 212–17.

11. Bill Powell and Rich Thomas, "The Raider: A Quick Fall from Grace" *Newsweek* (December 8, 1986): 66.

12. John Coyne, *Management Buyouts* (New York: Croomhelm, 1985), p. 61.

13. Russell Mitchell and Pete Engardio, "But Can He Handle an Ax?" *Business Week* (January 25, 1988): 35.

14. Billingham, "Hostile Corporate Takeovers," pp. 4–8.

15. Bruce Nussbaum, "Deal Mania—The Tempo Is Frantic and the Prosperity of the U.S. Is at Stake," *Business Week* (November 24, 1986): 75.

16. Ruth Simon, "Of Pots and Paintbrushes," *Forbes* (November 3, 1986): 75.

17. Thomas Murray, "Here Comes the 'Tin' Parachute," *Dun's Business Monthly* (January 1987): 62.

18. "Compromise Near in Delaware," *New York Times* (December 21, 1987): D2.

19. C. Yang and J. Weber, "Is Delaware about to Harpoon the Sharks?" *Business Week* (January 25, 1988): 34.

20. Joel Kotkin, "What I Do in Private Is My Own Business," *INC* (November 1986): 66.

21. Mercer, "Raiders Might Be after Your Company Next," p. 14.

22. Doug Bandow, "Are Hostile Takeovers Good for the Economy?" *Business and Society Review* (Fall 1987): 47.

23. Ibid.

24. Oscar S. Wyatt, Jr., "Acquisitions: Everyone Can and Should Benefit," *Industry Week* (September 30, 1985): 14.

25. Ajit Singh, *Takeover* (London: Cambridge University Press, 1971), pp. 20–22.

26. Alkhafaji, *Stakeholder Approach to Corporate Governance*, pp. 232–38.

27. Ronald Henkoff, "Deals of the Year," *Fortune* (January 30, 1989): 162–70.

28. Ibid.

29. Ibid.

30. Scharf, *Acquisitions, Mergers, Sales, and Takeovers*, pp. 159–70.

31. Ibid.

5

BUYOUTS

A recent trend in the business world is causing major restructuring of companies: an increasingly large number of companies are involved in mergers, takeovers, and buyouts. In fact, the number of takeovers, mergers, and acquisitions has increased to such a degree that "no one is safe."[1] Putting this in monetary terms, "the total value of American mergers and acquisitions for the 1988 year is more than 300 billion dollars."[2]

LEVERAGED BUYOUTS

A leveraged buyout (LBO) is a buyout in which a group of investors uses debt financing to buy a majority of the stock in a public company, thereby taking it private. LBOs are the hottest craze in finance in the United States today. If a company went private in the last several years, chances are good that it was done through an LBO.

There are many reasons why LBOs take place:

1. Management concentrates on cash flow and does not concern itself with stock market pressures and short-term earnings being reported. The focus is on long-term growth and profitability.
2. Managers become their own bosses. They can run the business the way they want to, reviving their entrepreneurial spirit.

3. Because of the financial structure that exists, management can pay off their debt and reenter the public market for an enormous profit, usually in about seven years.
4. LBOs eliminate the need to deal with security analysts.
5. LBOs eliminate thousands of shareholders with conflicting viewpoints.
6. LBOs eliminate the pressure to produce higher earnings every quarter.
7. Going private is easy.
8. LBOs increase the value of the stockholders' shares.
9. LBOs may prevent hostile takeovers.

Since the beginning of leveraged buyouts in the 1960s, they have become increasingly popular as a form of acquisition. In the 1970s, $3-billion worth of leveraged buyouts were concluded; by 1988, that total had ballooned to $39 billion, excluding the RJR Nabisco deal which exceeded $25 billion. The amount of money involved in LBOs sharply increased from $636 million in 1979 to $10.8 billion in 1984. Ellyn E. Spragins notes that "a few years ago it cost 9 to 10 times a company's earnings to buy it but now it takes 14 times the earnings or more."[3]

There is much that managers have to learn about the techniques and stages of these buyouts. The techniques utilized during and after leveraged buyouts not only enable managers to better handle public companies going private, but can also benefit managers in the public sector in their everyday functions.

One of the first concerns of LBOs is the management of the business's cash flow. When performing a leveraged buyout the firm will incur a substantial debt. Some people believe this to be a dangerous maneuver, but only a handful of companies have been overwhelmed by this debt. Managers contend that they can handle this debt unless the economy slides into a deep recession. More than likely, executives who run into trouble are incompetent at managing their cash flow. The same could be said about managers who run publicly held companies into bankruptcy.

The number of LBOs has increased at an amazing rate in the past few years and this trend shows no sign of slowing down. According to Alexander Taylor, in 1979 there were only 16 LBOs while in 1983 there were 36 buyouts worth several billion dollars. During the first quarter of 1983, 62 LBOs occurred which were valued in excess of $4.9 billion, while in 1984, there were 250 LBOs worth $18.6 billion.[4]

In the past two years Days Inn Corp., Safeways Inc., and American Standard have been taken over, borrowing huge sums to buy out shareholders. The largest LBO before November 1988 had been Montgomery Ward at $3.8 billion; Kroger Co. had been threatened by Kohlberg, Kravis, & Roberts with a $4.6-billion LBO.

In the first ten months of 1988, according to IDD Information Services, a Manhattan research firm, 143 companies were taken private in buyouts worth $91 billion, opposed to 105 deals worth $36 billion during the same period of 1987.[5] These transactions enrich shareholders and buyout specialists, but the takeovers could be causing grave damage to U.S. industry. Never before has debt been substituted for shareholders' equity on such a huge scale.

According to the *New York Times*, the number of attempted takeovers, mergers, and other restructurings has jumped sharply in recent days. As of April 11, 1989, P. A. Bergner bid $282 million for Carson Pirie Scott, NCNB offered $2.3 billion for Citizens and Southern, Beecham Group and Smith Kline Beckman said they might merge substantial parts of their businesses, and Harold C. Simmons, the Texas raider, disclosed that he owned large blocks of shares in Lockheed, Paccar, Phelps Dodge, and Chrysler.[6] It appears that the action is accelerating. And because there is so much money chasing the deals, Wall Street analysts expect the trend to continue.

TYPES OF BUYOUTS

In the 1980s it became quite popular for companies to use buyouts to get to more solvent financial ground. Buyouts are also used to seek organizational and structural changes.

The most popular type of buyout is the leveraged buyout (LBO). This is a deal financed mostly by debt in which investors contribute a small percentage of the purchase price and the remainder of the purchase is financed by loans secured from banks and sometimes insurance companies. The assets of the company being bought out are used as collateral, or leverage, against the debt bestowed upon them.

A second method of making a company private is the management buyout (MBO). This type of buyout occurs when management buys controlling interests of a public company and creates a private entity. Similar to LBOs, MBOs can be complex and may result in some form of leveraged financing.

A third buyout method is the spinoff (divestment). This occurs when employees of one company choose to establish a new firm using skills and capital previously acquired. Employees usually maintain a relationship with the previous employer. This type of buyout usually occurs when a firm's employees are highly entrepreneurial.

The final type of buyout is the employee stock ownership program (ESOP). This program allows employees to borrow money from the bank in order to buy back stocks from the company. An ESOP allows employees to have a role in corporate governance.

Certain groups of people stand to benefit from such acquisitions. Shareholders benefit by receiving a higher market value for their stock holdings in a corporation whenever it goes up for sale. Financial intermediaries benefit because the deal is financed through debt, usually through junk bonds which are high-risk and offer a higher than average return to investors. The corporation enjoys productivity increases; managers, faced with meeting interest payments, are forced to make the company more productive, usually by restructuring through downsizing.

LBO DEVELOPMENT

In the 1960s, many businesses decided to merge or acquire new businesses, but most of these buyouts were not successful. The effect of inflation upon the economy has been to increase the attractiveness of leveraged financing. The presence of inflation benefits debtors because it reduces the effective payment. This fact is fundamental to the success of LBOs. Corporations involved in LBOs, therefore, are helped by inflation to pay off the debt incurred in financing the acquisition. Cash savings have become particularly important today due to the rising costs of going private.

PUBLIC OPINION

A recent Harris Poll indicates that despite the continuing high rate of corporate mergers, six times as many Americans (49 percent as compared to 8 percent) think hostile takeovers do more harm than good to the economy.[7] At the core of public doubts about hostile takeovers is the widespread feeling that most critical interests, other than the price shareholders receive, are ignored. When asked to give a priority ranking of whose interests should be most protected in a hostile takeover, the public puts stockholders low on the list: employees' interests are seen as the top priority in takeovers, (cited by 47 percent), followed by the interests of the community in which the company is located (19 percent) and customers who depend on the products or services of the company (19 percent nationwide). In fourth place come stockholders, followed by the interests of top management.

A substantial majority (65 percent) of the public would favor Congress passing additional legislation closely regulating the ground rules for hostile takeovers. One specific proposal for legislation that meets with a 77 percent approval rate is that "all stockholders must receive an impact statement that would spell out how the takeover could affect employees, communities where the company is located, stockholders and the management."[8] One must search for moral principles that are inherently right or wrong apart from any particular circumstances. This case exemplifies moral principles which are (without other considerations) wrong under any circumstances. If these corporations applied their reasoning based on knowledge of prior experiences, they would be more reluctant to enter into such an arrangement, not only because of their duty and responsibility to the public, but also because of the effects they may have on society as well as the economy.

CHARACTERISTICS OF BUYOUT TARGETS

Companies involved in LBOs have certain features in common. Leonard Shaykin of Alder and Shaykin believes that consistent past profits, predictable future profits, and quality management control are vital to an attractive LBO target.[9] LBOs are also associated with mature companies in stable industries. Banks are unwilling to loan large amounts of money to a newly formed and unproven company. Any public operating company can request a leveraged buyout and for the most part, most businesses receive the aid needed to go private. In addition, attractive LBO targets are usually companies demonstrating little or no growth. A company which is growing spends much of its profits maintaining and continuing its growth. Therefore the money needed to accomplish an LBO is not available.

The characteristic features of target companies are financial. A company that is involved in a buyout is usually cash-rich. For example, Beatrice, at the time it was bought out, had approximately $125 million in cash and $5 billion in current assets.[10] Since only a small amount of money is needed to operate the company, the rest can be put toward the MBO. Also some of the assets of the company can be sold and put toward the acquisition price. This allows the company to borrow less and pay its debts off sooner.

The companies that are being bought out are generally mature and operate in stable industries. The managers of these companies are aggressive entrepreneurs and risk takers. In many buyouts the first obstacle that managers face is financing the enormous debt. Running the new company is another concern to the new managers. The company must be cash-rich and show little or no growth. In conclusion, the company must be strong and stable with sharp, aggressive management for a successful buyout to take place (for comparisons, see figures 5.1 and 5.2).

Companies suited to leveraged and management buyouts hold large market shares in low-growth industries such as food retailing. Com-

Figure 5.1
Comparison of Some Major Buyouts

COMPANY	CONDITION BEFORE BUYOUT	MONEY INVOLVED	HOW FINANCED	MGT STYLE	TYPE OF BUYOUT
Beatrice	Steady growth	$6 billion	Kehlbers, Kravis, Roberts	Entre-prenuer	LBO
Viacom Int.	Recorded 1st loss in 3 yrs.	$2.9 billion	Prior Earn-ings, Sale of assets.	Entre-prenuer	MBO
Dr. Pepper	Slow, takeover attempt, stable	$640 million	Sale of assests.	Entre-prenuer	MBO
Blue Bell	Takeover attempt, profit low.	$550 million	Managers	Entre-prenuer	MBO
Macy's	Stockholders second guessing management	$3.6 million	Goldman, Sachs, Co.	Entre-prenuer	MBO
Levi-Strauss	Stable growth	$2 billion	Haas Family	Family wants control	LBO
Metro-media	Steady growth	$1.3 billion	Institu-tional Investors	Entre-prenuer	MBO
Frontie Airlines	Losing money	$400 million	Banks	Entre-prenuer	MBO
Allen Bradley	Fair condition union problems	$1 billion	Forstmann, Little & Co.	Wanted more control	MBO
Safeway Stores	Takeover attempts	$4.1 billion	K,K, & R.	Entre-prenuer	MBO
Cole Nat Corp.	To Form a 2nd Toys 'R' Us	$320 million	K,K, & R.	Family owned	MBO
National Gypsum	Takeover attempts	$1.2 billion	Intitu-tional Investors	Entre-prenuer	LBO
Revlon	Poor Earnings		Junk Bonds	Entre-Prenuer	LBO
North-west Ind.	Slow	$1.4 billion	William Farley, Investors	Entre-prenuer	LBO
Lily - Tulip Inc	Losing money		K,K, & R	Entre-prenuer	MBO
RJR Nabisco	Slow Growth	$25 billion	K,K, & R	Entre-prenuer	LBO

Figure 5.2
Potential Buyout Targets

COMPANY	TYPE OF BUSINESS
1) Beatrice	Food
2) Viacom Int.	Broadcasting
3) Dr. Pepper	Soft-Drink
4) Blue Bell	Clothing
5) Macy's	Department Store
6) Levi-Strauss	Clothing
7) Metromedia	Broadcasting
8) Frontier Airlines	Airline Industry
9) Allen Bradley	Equipment Manufacturer
10) Safeway Stores	Drug Store
11) Cole Nat. Corp	Toy Store
12) National Gypsum	Housing Materials
13) Revlon	Cosmetics
14) Northwest Ind.	Consumer soft goods, batteries
15) Lily-Tulip Inc.	Cap Maker
16) RJR Nabisco	Tobacco products, foods

panies which go private often assume debt to equity ratios of 10 to 1 or even 20 to 1. In order to reduce high debt to equity ratios many companies are forced to streamline operations by selling off unnecessary assets and subsidiaries.

Managers are forced to stretch every dollar by reducing inventories and receivables, delaying the payment of bills, and reducing working capital. Propones of MBOs and LBOs assume that large debts are forcing managers to run companies efficiently and are eliminating a large portion of waste in American industry.

PROBLEMS WITH BUYOUTS

In most buyouts management's cash contribution is a relatively small proportion of the total purchase price; the balance of the funding is provided by loans from financial institutions and banks.

A management buyout is different from any other acquisition as far as tax considerations are concerned. In these transactions, the parent firm effectively takes on the past tax history of its new subsidiary when it buys the shares. The parent company (or its advisors) should investigate the company's tax position to determine whether tax liabilities may arise as a result of technical factors and at higher rates than anticipated in the profit and cash forecasts.

In most buyouts trading operations which were formerly carried out by a subsidiary of a large company are now carried out in a smaller and financially weaker entity. The potential implications of this must be anticipated before the buyout occurs.

Competitors often try to suggest to customers that the company's viability is now suspect and may, by very aggressive pricing, force the newly purchased company out of the market. Customers may respond by changing suppliers or reducing their requirements.

Suppliers may be concerned about the credit worthiness of the new business and may arbitrarily and suddenly withdraw credit facilities or restrict the level of supply, at least until they are satisfied with the stability of the company.

Both of these problems can have disastrous effects on cash flow in the early stages of the buyout. Managers should make sure that key customers and suppliers are aware of what is occurring and of the strength of the financial support for the new vendors. It is also highly desirable to allow a sufficient cushion within the funding of the company for the buyout target to be able to weather a temporary problem.

ENTREPRENEURIAL LEVERAGED BUYOUTS

Many entrepreneurs establish themselves by building a new business from scratch and working to remain solvent and earn a profit. However, there is another kind of entrepreneur who acquires an already-established business. This is known as an entrepreneurial leveraged buyout (E-LBO). The difference between the two is that an E-LBO involves the buying-out of a company whose profits are known whereas the establishment of a new company, by entrepreneurs, involves a much higher risk. The financing of both, however, is a major factor.

FINANCIAL INSTITUTIONS AND THE ENTREPRENEUR

Institutions are willing to help finance E-LBOs due to the fact that the risk is much lower than the financing of new ventures. Institutional lenders are aware of the fact that entrepreneurs are likely to be educated and knowledgeable about the field into which they are buying. Also, the major investors are likely to be wealthy, thus reinforcing their success and reassuring the lender. An institutional lender feels safer about investing his money in an E-LBO when the entrepreneur himself is making a large contribution.

Another characteristic of institutional lenders is that they are likely to provide long repayment periods. This is due to the confidence that lenders gain in the E-LBOs. They do not feel a need to demand the money in a short period of time because the company is unlikely to have any great cash flow in the starting stages. In this way, leverage financers earn more interest over the longer repayment period.

One of the major investment banking firms in New York City is Forstmann Little & Co. They have financed such buyouts as Revlon, Dr. Pepper Co., and Allen-Bradley Co. Lending companies such as these help out E-LBOs. In order to feel even safer about their investment, they often seek to secure loans with personal guarantees, especially when the amount is substantial.

Another characteristic of institutional lenders is that they charge a much lower interest rate to E-LBOs than charged to nonentrepreneurial LBO investors. This is due to the previously stated facts that lenders are confident because of stable industry, established companies, and respected investors.

As we have seen, institutional lenders find it more profitable to invest in E-LBOs than in new ventures. It is an advantage for them to know the history of the entrepreneur in order to ensure the safety of their money. This is a sort of reciprocal arrangement because lenders are confident in their investment in E-LBOs while entrepreneurs receive the loan with a low interest rate.

INTERNATIONAL BUYOUTS

Aside from being one of America's favorite business strategies, LBOs are becoming very popular in international business as well. U.S. investors had such an effect that they helped push the dollar amount of LBOs from $400,000 in 1984 to approximately $1.3 million in 1985.

The political effects of this U.S. push resulted in opposition to foreign bidders. Despite this opposition, U.S. influence continues to rise in Great Britain. The United States did have concerns about the long-run economic prospects, but the current booming market is tempting enough to draw investors' attention.

International leveraged buyouts are very much like U.S. leveraged buyouts in that a firm is taken over by outsiders separate from the company proper. International takeovers are a form of involvement which typically appeals to the firm which has had prior international experience and which seeks to obtain a business relative to the firm's core operations. Few companies are willing to commit a substantial portion of their resources to foreign operations in the initial stages of international operations. For that matter, they may not even have the resources sufficient to expand abroad.

A major motive for seeking an acquisition is that a potential investor may find it difficult to either transfer some resource to a foreign operation or to acquire the resource (labor/personnel) locally for a new facility. The desire for greater growth in a shorter time period is another factor which entices a firm to seek an existing firm. Oligopoly considerations can also influence acquisition activity within highly concentrated industries. Yet another reason for a firm wanting to acquire another is that companies from countries with relatively low-cost capital will value foreign earnings from operations above domestic financial markets. The lower capital costs reflect lower discount rates which result in higher net value estimates. Finally, it may save a firm money if it buys an existing firm because this possibly provides a company with brand identification and a sort of goodwill which could be very costly to develop in a foreign country. Acquisitions reduce costs and risks as well as provide quicker results. This has been seen as a way of becoming a part of a foreign market without adding capacity to that market.

One of the most important concerns of international acquisition is the management style the acquiring firm practices. If management assumes a passive role, expecting the firm to basically take care of itself, financial troubles will surface. If this situation arises, it has been argued, then incentives for the affiliate to match its former performance are reduced. Management may no longer have the same incentive to perform under the new arrangement as it did when the company was more independent. Problems arise when the management team is replaced or when the foreign firm attempts to standardize the existing personnel, facilities, and systems to conform to global standards. This, then, can be more time consuming, costly, and problematic than starting anew. Another major flaw in acquiring a firm is that the implementation of information and control systems often can be a difficult process. Management's attitudes and incentives are often less constructive in an acquired company.

Currently, the United States is experiencing a high rate of foreign acquisitions. The following are some of the reasons for these acquisitions:

1. low stock prices
2. large amounts of cash
3. the falling value of the dollar
4. recent economic recovery in Europe

Although there have been quite a number of successful international buyouts, there appears to be a 50 percent failure rate of U.S. acquisitions of foreign firms. The reasons are as follows:

1. Unfamiliar customers and technology
2. Foreign firms which are much less similar to U.S. companies than appear on the surface
3. Low payoffs in comparison with other methods of market penetration
4. Tendency to acquire unprofitable enterprises in the belief these firms can be turned around under new management

In sum, when deciding which form of international business a firm should adopt, several factors must be taken into account. These include the legal environment, cost, experience, competition, risk, control, and the nature of the assets. After taking the above factors into consideration, the choice among licensing, joint ventures, and wholly owned subsidiaries can be structured within a portfolio perspective.

MANAGEMENT BUYOUTS

From its small beginnings before 1980, the buyout marketplace developed rapidly, so that by 1985 it was estimated by the Centre for Management Buyout Research that some 229 buyouts took place. Today, buyouts are an important feature of our economy. Having only tentatively appeared on the corporate scene in the late 1970s, they have become, in less than a decade, well established means by which a transfer of company ownership is effected. The essential characteristics of management buyouts are that the company is purchased by its current management, which has a significant equity stake in the company postbuyout, that the company becomes a private independent company, and that the funding generally leaves the company in a highly geared position.

LEGISLATION

According to professor of philosophy Virginia Held, the set of rights implied in the concept of property comprises the rights to possess, use, manage, dispose of, and restrict others' access to things.[11] Property implies asset of interests in the sense that if our possessions become worthless we no longer have property. Today's capitalistic society supports this viewpoint. It has been noted that the bulwark of capitalism is the claim that we have a moral right to property. In fact, capitalism is a specific form of private property.[12]

Capitalism can be defined as an economic system in which the major portion of production and distribution is in private hands, operating under what is termed a profit or market system. The U.S. economy is the world's leading capitalist economy. This means all manufacturing firms are privately owned, including those that produce military hardware for the government. The same applies to banks, insurance companies, and most transportation companies. All businesses and power companies are also privately owned.

These privately owned interests determine supply by consumer demand. With the exception of government expenditures for such things as health, education, welfare, highways, and military equipment, no central governing body dictates to these private owners what or how much will be produced. Hence, the English philosopher John Locke expressed what has become a basic tenet of capitalism: that property ownership is a moral right.[13]

Companies have duties that must be observed, such as providing customers with the best possible products, at the best possible prices, in the most efficient manner. This is the "ought," the duty. Consumers are entitled to high-quality products and services at a reasonably fair price.

This is no longer the "greatest total goods" principle. The facts are that consumers pay dearly for monopolized market control. Once a few firms gain a monopoly position in a product category, the market for that category is considered to be mature and the companies are able to push up prices. Shared monopolies are the major cause of inflation in our economy. (Now how can this be a "willing of the good" or something good in and of itself?) We also know that corporations are operated by financial managers interested only in corporate growth—not in what is best for society as a whole.

MANAGEMENT BENEFITS

A substantial advantage to going private is the ability to turn a company around and go public again. Some buyout deals get paid off in time and companies are owned free and clear. But often more debt is assumed to make acquisitions and many bought-out companies go public again, scoring a second success in the new issues market.

The benefits to management are the ability to "own" their own company without direction from any elected board of directors. Without shareholders looking at quarterly profit statements, managers can focus on long-term profit goals more in keeping with their new financial liabilities. With more at stake personally, management will truly have to keep their heads up and hone their business skills.

Lastly, benefits such as increased career opportunities, increased security of supply, and increased economic opportunities in the surrounding community are found in takeovers.[14]

THE ROLE OF THE BOARD OF DIRECTORS

The board of directors has a responsibility to protect the interests of shareholders in the event of a buyout. They should let shareholders know the true value of their shares before the buyout. They must also make the best decisions about the LBO from the point of view of the stockholders. If they do not, "the board and management of the company are going to hear from the stockholders, who will vote with their feet and get out of the stock."[15]

The board of directors is obligated to the stakeholders of the company. Employees, creditors, suppliers, and customers have made a large investment in the company. These groups have an enduring relationship with the company and should have some recognition. In fact the corporate charter details responsibility to stakeholders.

TAX ADVANTAGES

The tax laws in the United States encourage LBOs because they permit investors to deduct interest on the debts they have incurred. The money that would have gone to pay taxes can instead be used to pay off the loan. The tax advantage of Norris Industries amounted to a $76-million decrease in taxable income. If a tax rate of 50 percent is used, this leaves Norris with a $38-million savings. That amount was more than 60 percent of its interest payments in 1987.[16] Benton Malkiel of Vale suggests that U.S. tax laws "clearly encourage this kind of activity."[17]

Furthermore, the accounting procedures for such an acquisition of a company's assets can be represented at market price. The worth of tangible assets can be represented at market price. Due to the increased value of the asset, the depreciation on that asset can be increased which in turn decreases the company's taxable income.

THE FUTURE OF TAKEOVERS, MERGERS, AND LBOs

Some doom sayers believe that, like all investment trends, leveraged buyouts will eventually be carried to excess. In their greed, investors will start reaching for the marginal deals. Other brokers will find a way to bring the public in at an early stage when the risk is still high. There will be failures and scandals and big loan losses, and the whole game will be given a bad name.

Corporate buyers, heartened by the favorable outlooks on economic and interest rates, should stay busy, as individual raiders are hurt by judicial and legislative antitakeover moves. Experts predict that cash tender offers are still the best bet to overcome toughened takeover defenses, and will become increasingly popular. Foreign investment in U.S. firms will remain keen; for the first time in years, U.S. suitors are seeking European targets, due to the upcoming 1992 Common Market consolidation.[18]

In the United States, property ownership is as important as the rights of life, liberty, and free expression. So entrenched are cultural assumptions about private property that few of us ever question the extent of this right, or whether it is, in fact, a moral right, and if so, why. Clearly, the American people feel that the spate of corporate takeovers is an alarming development, and they want government to set new ground rules changing the priorities which ought to be given consideration.

The wave of leveraged buyouts is clearly weakening the competitiveness of many U.S. companies that have fought so hard to regain it. Consumers pay for needless costs directly in the form of higher prices and indirectly in the form of reduced competition. Obviously, a reevaluation of this system is desperately needed.

NOTES

1. Peter Newcomb, "No One Is Safe," *Forbes* (July 13, 1987): 121.

2. Richard I. Kirkland, Jr., "Merger Mania is Sweeping Europe," *Fortune International* (December 19, 1988): 42.

3. Ellyn E. Spragins, "Leveraged Buyouts Aren't Just for Daredevils Anymore," *Business Week* (August 11, 1986): 50.

4. Gary Weiss, "ABC's of LBOs: What Makes Leveraged Buyouts Popular," *Barron's* (August 19, 1985).

5. Bill Saporito, "Who Wins in the Hugest Deals," *Fortune* (November 21, 1988): 49–50.

6. Anise C. Wallace, "Merger Activity Accelerating," *New York Times* (April 11, 1989): 24.

7. Louis Harris, "Public Sees More Harm Than Good in Corporate Takeovers," *The Harris Poll* (February 10–14, 1980): 14.

8. Ibid.

9. John Greenwald, "The Popular Game of Going Private," *Time* (November 4, 1985): 55.

10. *Moody's Industrial Manual*, Volume 1, A–1, Moody's Investors Service, Inc., New York, 1985, p. 2609.

11. Virginia Held, *Property, Profits, and Economic Justice* (Belmont, Calif.: Wadsworth, 1980), pp. 1–3.

12. Vincent Barry, *Moral Issues in Business*, 3d ed. (Belmont, Calif.: Wadsworth, 1986), p. 84.

13. Ibid., p. 79.

14. Oscar S. Wyatt, Jr., "Acquisitions: Everyone Can and Should Benefit," *Industry Week* (September 30, 1985): 14.

15. Ibid.

16. Susan D. Harding, Leon Hanouille, Joseph C. Rue, and Ara C. Volkan, "Why LBOs are Popular," *Management Accounting* (December 1985): 52.

17. Ibid.

18. Brooks Tigner, "Brussels Drafting One-Stop Shopping Rules for Growing Wave of European Takeovers," *International Management* (October 1988).

6

MANAGEMENT BUYOUTS

During the late 1960s and early 1970s, there was an overabundance of new issue stocks in the stock market. In 1974 the stock market declined considerably; the Dow Jones Industrial average, which had risen to 1036 points in 1972, dropped to 578 points.[1] The newly issued stocks were hit hardest. Their values plunged along with the rest of the market. For these troubled companies being public had lost its appeal because stockholders were no longer interested in investing. In 1975, in order to restructure, several companies went private. Management turned to public stockholders and declared that the public stock would be bought back. Unfortunately for stockholders and outside investors there was no chance for others to bid; thus in most cases the buyout price given to shareholders was not fair. In response to this action, SEC declared that an acceptable MBO had to achieve something more than a blatant freezeout of public shareholders, that it had to satisfy some business purpose.[2]

REASONS FOR MANAGEMENT BUYOUTS

There are several reasons why management buyouts occur. First of all, a management buyout is an escape from the grasp of stockholders. After a buyout, the existing management no longer has to satisfy the stockholders' desire for short-term earning reports. Instead, management can concentrate on cash flow and long-term growth. Monitoring cash flow is important since management must produce a profit in order to survive and to pay off debt. For example, Axia, a diversified industrial products company, did just that. According to the chief executive Dennis W. Sheehan, "as a public company we generated cash that just sat there as excess working capital—some $40 million worth. There's no longer any excess; it goes to pay down the debt."[3]

Another reason management buyouts occur is that management can run its business in the most profitable way. As profit-seeking entrepreneurs, management shops around for the lowest priced goods and services. Any savings are realized as extra cash flow in the form of profits or debt-reducing money. Entrepreneurs are careful about costs. Extra expenses come out of management's pockets. Sheehan notes that "for executives of public companies, it is always so easy to grab a cab—or the corporate jet—at company expense. Once you're a manager-owner, you may walk the seven blocks or take Peoples Express."[4]

Hostile takeovers can be moderately reduced by MBOs. In fact, in 1983 top executives of Signode Corp., a packaging-materials manufacturer, repelled a hostile takeover by financier Victor Posner. The stumbling block of Posner's attempt was a $430-million management buyout.[5] Another example of a hostile takeover attempt blocked by a management buyout is the Uniroyal case. At Uniroyal's annual meeting in the spring of 1985, Carl Icahn proposed a takeover. As a result, Uniroyal hastily went private. Later Joseph P. Flannery, chief executive of Uniroyal, commented, "We had talked about private ownership in a general way previously, but frankly I think we were too conservative to have taken the risk of a leveraged buyout on our own initiative."[6]

In a buyout, management becomes an active member on both sides of the table. It acts on behalf of the shareholders to determine whether a sale is in their best interest and seeks the best possible price. It also acts on its own behalf as a profit-seeking entrepreneur. The morality of such a transaction has been questioned, but one thing is certain: the stockholders stand to gain a hefty profit. Investment bankers play a key role in defining the premium price that must be offered to persuade stockholders to part with their shares.

Using its entrepreneurial skills, management concentrates on long-term growth and profit after the buyout takes place. While the company is private, management improves the company's health, thus hoping that within several years the company will be able to once again go public. For example, in 1982 a Simon-led group of investors bought the Gibson greeting-card company from RCA for $1 million of its own money and $79 million of borrowed money. The investors then reorganized the private company. Just 18 months later, they sold $290 million of the company's stock to the public. When a company is reorganized properly by management, the result can be lucrative.[7]

ORGANIZATIONAL STRUCTURE AND BUYOUTS

Management stands to gain a great deal from a buyout. The most obvious benefit is job retention. Second, management becomes its own boss since it directly owns the company. Third, managers have the opportunity to develop a greater range of skills. As entrepreneurs, managers can contribute their expertise more than they could have when the company was public. Fourth, since the company does not have to report to the public (shareholders), there is a reduction in overhead office costs. Finally, since there is more emphasis on long-term investments, there is a possibility for more expenditures for research and development. Furthermore, for the company to be competitive, emphasis is placed on "special research"—new product development. In the Signode buyout, "instead of spending 70% of development funds on refining existing products, Signode will pump at least half of the R&D budget into a new product-development effort headed by several of its most talented engineers."[8]

In spite of all the gains, management can also lose in an MBO. Since there are no public funds (no stocks), management must resort to private borrowing. Not only does management have to worry about debt, but in the event of a failure or bankruptcy management will be unable to pay its debt. Furthermore, while management is burdened by debt, many creditors, suppliers, and customers place restrictions on the creditors of the private company. Finally, conflict can erupt. Because there are several bosses, conflicts of interest can cause problems.

Buyouts, however, offer management more gains than losses—hence their attractiveness. In fact, buyouts in the 1970s averaged around $3 million. Today, it is not unusual to have buyouts of $1 to 2 billion. Dollar volume has sharply increased. In 1980 volume was $1 billion; in 1984 it was $10.8 billion. In 1985, R. H. Macy's top officers offered $3.58 billion to buy out the company. Incidentally, this single management buyout was equal to one-third of the volume of the previous year.[9]

The management buyout of today focuses on companies in the mature stage of the business life-cycle. Demand is beginning to level off, growth is minimal, and the company is just about to enter the saturation stage. The majority of companies in this stage do not focus on new product development or extensive research. Since companies with huge growth require tremendous cash outlays for research and development, low-growth companies are prime buyout targets because they can quickly liquidate assets. For example, Albert J. Dunlap achieved great success for Lilly-Tulip Inc. after being appointed president following a loss of $11 million as a result of going private. Dunlap cut out $50 million in overhead. At the same time, he reduced the debt, upgraded the product, and received a profit of $8 million.[10]

Nukote, a manufacturer of ribbons for typewriters and computer printers, had trouble with its corporate parent; Unisys. After years of declining profits due to aging product lines, the management of Nukote bought the company for $60 million. After creating new product lines, overall rates grew 17 percent in 1988 to $150 million. Analysts say that Nukote was at its prime for a management buyout.

People have many different views of management buyouts and their benefits to the economy, to the country, and to stakeholders. Each buyout occurs for different reasons. For Todd C. Seltz, the opportunity to own and manage his own company free of corporate constraints proved to be the motivating factor in his decision for a management buyout. Seltz is currently the president and CEO of O. M. Scott & Son Company in Marysville, Ohio. With the help of Clayton & Dubiller, Inc., in December 1986, he and members of his management team bought the firm from ITT Corporation for $150 million. Seltz, Scott managers, and other investors combined their assets for a downpayment of $25 million for ITT. After the buyouts, Scott had a large amount of debt. Still Seltz is satisfied with managing his own company as an independent corporation.

According to Edward Weinstein, when O. M. Scott was a subsidiary of ITT, Seltz's major concern was to provide long-term growth. This was not taking place even though everyone was struggling to meet their objectives within ITT.[11]

Also at that time, there was a constant stream of negative publicity about buyouts. One of the major concerns was employees. How would they react? O. M. Scott had been an independent company for over one hundred years when it was acquired by ITT. Immediately, there was a negative reaction to the purchase because the company would now be controlled from New York City. For many years there had been a feeling that the control of the company was taken from the Marysville plant and placed in the hands of people who did not understand the business. But following the buyout, Seltz decided that the company and existing management would remain in Marysville. He stated, "I believe this produced a very positive feeling among employees and the community. It was almost like we were going back to the good old days—local management paying attention to local conditions."[12] Now management is happy and the community is benefiting because the company headquarters is stationed in its town. In addition, more jobs are open and prosperous economic conditions prevail.

Scott Seltz could not achieve growth until the buyout. He explains,

"All of those things could be accomplished within a large corporate structure, but things just get overweighted, overstuffed, and overscrutinized in a large company."[13] He is convinced that people have a strong desire to grow, and must be properly challenged and supported.

According to Seltz, the most difficult challenge the group faced was to believe that the company really was operating in a new and different environment and anything they did was subject to scrutiny.[14] If the management would like to serve the best interests of the business in the future, it must proceed forward and continue trusting its judgment.

When negotiating begins for a buyout, the stock of the company being pursued increases in value. This should encourage investment in the company. Also, current shareholders could receive a price for their stock that is above current market price. If the stockholders are happy, the tension of the buyout is eased. The community is more likely to help a company since they perceive growth and stability in the company. After the buyout, it usually takes anywhere from five to ten years to pay off the debt. Finally, enormous profits can be realized. In most cases, many stakeholders benefit from management buyout whereas, in hostile takeovers, there seems to be very little concern for society outside the company. Sheer profit is the motive.

The government is fairly lenient when it comes to tax laws regulating buyout activity. According to the U.S. tax code, most corporations are permitted to deduct the interest on debt and use the cash for payment purposes. At the time of buyout, most companies' assets would be equal to the current value which denotes a tax saving. Not only does the buyer benefit, but the seller as well.

THE ROLE OF ESOPS IN MBOS

Financing is a vital aspect of an MBO because without the proper backing, the MBO will not get off the ground. Without getting into the tax law of MBO financing as a whole, it is sufficient to say that management buys back the stockholders' shares and finances the buyout through tax-generated cash flows from principal and interest deductions of assets which are valued above the depreciated values on the books. One of the most effective and steadily increasing forms of financing are ESOPs. The employee stock ownership program was developed by Louis Kelso fifty years ago. He believed that the U.S. economy could not survive unless company employees held a significant equity stake in it.

ESOPs received a big boost in 1974 from the Employee Retirement Income Security Act. This act established tax breaks designed to encourage companies to set up retirement plans in which workers could share in the equity of the company. However, managers view ESOPs as a means for reducing the cost of capital, enlarging their own share of the new company, and a means of being able to pay top dollar, due to the fact that ESOPs can be persuaded to pay a higher price per share.

Basically, an ESOP is a trust created for the exclusive benefit of employees. The shares acquired by the ESOP are allocated to employees based on a plan and may be redeemed or cashed in by employees upon retirement for their market value. Corporations finance ESOPs through two main strategies. The corporation makes tax-deductible contributions to the ESOP and the funds are then used to buy corporate shares. Recent legislation, such as the Economic Recovery Tax Act (1981), permits tax deductions for corporations which contribute up to 25 percent of the employee payroll annually to the plan. The second way in which corporations finance buyouts through ESOPs is borrowing. ESOPs have become a major device for sheltering the operating income of a new company. The company borrows money from a commercial lender and loans the money to the ESOP which uses it to purchase corporate stock. Currently, the Internal Revenue Code allows generous deductions for contributions to repay the principal as well as the interest on the loan from the commercial lender.

An ESOP's tax structure not only provides management with the opportunity to take part in the entrepreneurial dream which motivates this nation, but it also enables commercial lenders to share tax breaks as well. ESOPs have created a broader market for banks, as approximately 40 percent are leveraged and rely on bank loans. An ESOP loan is perhaps safer than a regular corporate loan because the ESOP loan is being repaid with pretax dollars and less earnings are needed to pay back the debt. The Deficit Reduction Act of 1984 was a major force in bringing the ESOP market to commercial banks. First, it allowed stockholders to sell their shares to the ESOP, reinvest the proceeds in another corporation, and pay tax on the sale of the original stock only to the extent that the proceeds of the original sale exceeded the cost of replacement stock. Second, a corporation is permitted to deduct the amount of dividends paid on ESOP stock. Finally, commercial lenders are able to exclude 50 percent of the interest earned on an ESOP loan. This was the most attractive provision for the bank.[15]

ESOPs are not without their drawbacks. There are substantial administrative costs and the extensive use of corporate funds. Also, there must be a large employee base to warrant such a purchase of ownership interests.

ESOPs have powerful opponents. Employee benefits are constantly questioned by participants and society alike, but no voice is louder than that of the U.S. Department of Labor. One example of how the department is ensuring that all parties receive a fair deal is illustrated in the Scott & Fetzer Co. case. Under its scheme, shareholders were to receive

$62 a share. The ESOP was to receive 41 percent of the company, management 29 percent, and the chief lender 30 percent. The buyout was to consist of $407 million from the bank, $15 million from management, and $152 million from company cash. The Department of Labor rejected the plan on the grounds that management came off too well in the deal while the ESOP would receive too small a share of the company for what it risked.

It is clear how the new tax law will affect the future of ESOPs and their role in MBOs. However, debt will still be a less expensive form of finance for companies than equity since interest costs are deductible while dividends are not.

CHARACTERISTICS OF MBOS

A company being considered for a management buyout should have the following characteristics:

1. Maturity
2. An established cash flow
3. A heavy asset base (i.e., manufacturing equipment fully depreciated)
4. Stable and strong product line
5. Strong management with entrepreneurial tendencies
6. Low current and long-term debt
7. No legal problems (creditors)
8. Dominant market position (niche)
9. Decent growth prospects

Although similar characteristics are associated with management buyouts, the objectives of management teams differ depending on each situation. Some management teams undertake buyouts in order to gain control and keep the company intact. Other buyouts are initiated to prevent hostile takeovers; after such a transaction parts of the company are quickly liquidated.

The following three companies were chosen to illustrate examples of management buyouts. Each have many of the necessary characteristics for a management buyout, but they all have unique goals and objectives.

R. H. Macy and Company, Inc.

In October 1985, the senior executives of R. H. Macy and Company, Inc., proposed a leveraged buyout of the company for $3.7 billion. President Edward S. Finklestein claimed the purpose of the buyout was to free the company's management from the pressures of short-term financial gains that are typically imposed on a publically owned company. As a privately owned company, Macy's would not be required to report its financial status or pay dividends to its public stockholders. Taking the company private would have many benefits for management. Although more than one hundred managers would be involved, each would be increasing his or her share of ownership, receiving incentive and motivation for improved performance. In the past, Macy's had lost several top managers to competitors. This management buyout would keep talented executives in the company.

Approximately $600 million in financing for the buyout was provided by the managers and the remainder came from backers such as Citibank, Manufacturer's Hanover Trust Company, and General Electric Credit Corporation. Finklestein said that the company would continue its long-term expansion strategies while improving the quality of service and selling more private label merchandise.[16] Macy's should be able to budget funds more freely as a private company in order to generate greater customer satisfaction and a competitive edge. However, a large debt makes geographical expansion and increasing budgets very difficult to finance. Also, the management must realize that they will not be independent as long as they have obligations to equity partners who will undoubtedly be keeping a close eye on them.

As of October 5, 1986, Macy's subsidiary, Bamberger's, was known as Macy's. This change reflected the new top management's desire for a more centralized operation. Bamberger's corporate division was renamed Macy's of New Jersey. Also, the new management decided to sell off nine of its shopping malls for approximately $500 million. These nine shopping malls contained Macy's stores which would continue to operate after the malls were sold. Macy's would use the money obtained from sales to help finance the debt incurred in the $3.7-billion buyout.

ARA Services of Philadelphia

ARA Services provides food and refreshment services in sports stadiums, school and business cafeterias, and airports; it also provided these services at the last three Olympic Games. It is a *Fortune* 500 company with over 130,000 client organizations. In December 1984, the company went through a leveraged buyout. Eighty-seven of the company's top managers made an offer of nearly $890 million that was approved by the board of directors. This same group had offered to buy the company in mid-September of the same year for $874 million, but that offer was rejected. Also, in July 1984, former ARA executive William Siegel led a group of investors in an offer of $720 million, but that, too, was rejected.

ARA decided to become private in order to preserve its values. Management did not want to change the company, but wished to maintain its spirit, momentum, and commitment to quality service.[17]

WEIRTON STEEL OF WEST VIRGINIA

Another company with a success story following a switch from public to private is Weirton Steel. On January 11, 1984, an ESOP was set up for the purchase of a division of National Steel in Weirton, West Virginia. Weirton's 8,500 employees were all shareholders in the company. Weirton was the largest industrial ESOP in the nation.[18] The employees had to take a 20 percent cut in wages and benefits plus a six-year wage freeze. But the ESOP gave employees a share in the profits—$152 million in almost three years. Employees receive one-third of Weirton's profits when its equity reaches $100 million, and one-half when it reaches $250 million.[19]

Union and nonunion leaders meet once a month to discuss the performance of Weirton.[20] Weirton has taken great strides to make the employees an important part of the company and respects their role as owners. This respect has led the company to enjoy large profits while other steel companies are faltering.

A switch from being a public to a private corporation can be profitable. Management buyouts which keep the current employee base and the company intact usually benefit all parties involved. This is in contrast to those buyouts which are organized in an effort to avoid hostile takeovers. These buyouts often result in rapid divestitures, where managers collect large profits while employees are losing their jobs. One must question the integrity of management's motives in these deals. It is also apparent that management buyouts may be subject to impending lawsuits from shareholders who are reluctant to give up their interest in a company. Lawsuits may be brought by employees who fear losing their salaries and/or benefits from an unscrupulous buyout.

EVALUATION

The future of management buyouts is hard to predict. Banks will probably have even stricter regulations for investors in buyouts. For example, if a bank lends $50 million to a firm and the firm goes bankrupt, the bank probably will not receive the money it previously lent. More government regulations will also be imposed. Many states will probably develop their own laws concerning buyouts. Wisconsin law, for example, requires a bidder that acquires 10 percent or more of a target company's shares to wait three years or have the approval of the company's directors in order to complete the merger. This law effectively eliminates hostile leveraged buyouts. At present thirty states of the fifty have passed various takeover laws; many are similar to Wisconsin's. About 784 of the country's 1,000 largest companies are in states with laws similar to Wisconsin's.[21]

Economic aspects of MBOs will be researched even more in the future. The debt of the buyout will help the economy if the interest rates are down and hurt businesses if sales decline or inflation goes up. It will help keep the economy prosperous by circulating money. Perhaps management buyout will create powerful incentives for entrepreneurship.

Another issue in future management buyouts concerns employees. One of the main concerns of the employees from top-level management to blue-collar workers is whether they will be laid off as a result of buyout. Whenever the issue of a buyout arises, people become so concerned that productivity may be reduced. They may begin to feel insecure about their jobs. Stress from worry can create an unhappy family and home life. People could lose complete trust in companies that participate in any kind of acquisition, and if not carefully monitored, people might be the biggest obstacle in being scrutinized. This action could lead to a decline in the number of skilled and nonskilled workers and in the company's future. The economy of the company could be reduced due to the lack of skilled employees.

Over time, the buyout market has greatly changed, especially in the last decade. It will continue to change as more people learn how to arrange deals and profit from them. Boards of directors must protect their stockholders from inadequate bids. These leaders must also prevent their companies from becoming vulnerable or making aimless buyouts. Most of all, management should protect its stakeholders.

At this point in time, management buyouts have been generally profitable and successful. However, the real test of this form of ownership will come when the economic tides change.

NOTES

1. Louis Lowestein, "Management Buyouts," *Columbia Law Review* 85 (1983): 732.

2. Ibid., p. 733.

3. Maggie McComas, "Life Isn't Easy," *Fortune* (December 9, 1985): 43–47.

4. Ibid., p. 44.

5. Wm. Franklin McMahon, "How Signode's Managers Turned into Entrepreneurs," *Business Week* (June 6, 1983): 86–88.

6. McComas, "Life Isn't Easy," p. 43.

7. John Greenwald, "The Popular Game of Going Private," *Time* (November 4, 1985): 54–55.

8. McMahon, "Signode's Managers," p. 86.

9. Greenwald, "Popular Game," p. 56.

10. Abbass F. Alkhafaji, *A Stakeholder Approach to Corporate Governance: Managing in a Dynamic Environment* (New York: Quorum, 1989).

11. Edward Weinstein, "Why I Bought the Company," *Journal of Business Strategy* (January–February 1989): 5.

12. Ibid., p. 6.

13. Ibid.

14. Ibid.

15. Sheila C. Turpin-Forster, "ESOPs Mean Business," *ABA Banking Journal* (October 1985): 164.

16. "Top Executives Offer to Buy Macy's," *New York Times* (October 22, 1985): A1.

17. Taken from 1986 ARA Services report to employees, p. 2.

18. Matt Bulvony, "Making Money—and History—at Weirton," *Business Week* (November 12, 1984): 136.

19. Ibid.

20. Ibid.

21. Stephen Wermiel, "Supreme Court Declines to Review Law in Wisconsin Curbing Hostile Takeovers," *Wall Street Journal* (November 7, 1989):6–17.

BIBLIOGRAPHY

Berger, Joan, and Norman Jonas. "Do These Deals Help or Hurt the United States Economy?" *Business Week* (November 24, 1986): 86.

Block, Stanley B. "Buy-Sell Agreements for Privately Held Corporations." *Journal of Accountancy* (September 1985): 114.

Dobrzynski, Judith H. "More Than Ever, It's Management for the Short Term." *Business Week* (November 24, 1986): 92.

Nussbaum, Bruce. "Deal Mania—The Tempo Is Frantic and the Prosperity of the U.S. Is at Stake." *Business Week* (November 24, 1986): 75.

7

MANAGEMENT'S PERCEPTION
OF BUYOUTS

The buyout phenomenon that has revolutionized the ways that companies merge, acquire other companies, and at times see themselves being swallowed up is particularly attractive to managers within companies and the new breed of entrepreneurs. Companies use buyouts to transform themselves into more solvent financial entities as well as to seek changes in organization and structure. Being taken private in the buyout process results in the company no longer having to concentrate on short-term strategies designed to keep shareholders content. It may now develop strategic plans that focus on long-term growth and profitability. The question of repaying the resulting debt from the buyout becomes an urgent one that successful buyout engineers must answer in order to remain in business and avoid a buyout or takeover by others both within and outside the company.

A buyout is attractive to managers because it enables them to take the company private, hold ultimate control and decision-making responsibility, and directly participate in the profits the company generates. While the managers are also directly responsible for the large debt created, they more than any others should be able to guide the company to maximum growth and profitability since they know the company operations best and recognize what steps must be taken.

Entrepreneurs, who once built ventures from scratch, are turning to the buyout as a means of acquiring an already established company that they envision as having growth and expansion as well as profitability potential. This method of entrepreneurship is often greeted with more enthusiasm on the part of banks and venture capitalists in providing funds and alleviates the need to "reinvent the wheel" as much of the technology and procedures are already in place in the buyout target.

THE POPULARITY AND BENEFITS OF BUYOUTS

Buyouts are growing in popularity. This is because the leveraging (debt) technique involves both the acquiring of a company and the refinancing of that company through debt, partially secured by company assets. While this results in a higher degree of financial risk for purchasers and financiers, the purchaser must contribute a relatively minimal amount of personal cash to the total purchase price. This is very attractive to managers and entrepreneurs who do not have the large cash reserves necessary for traditional acquisition measures.

Buyouts are seen by many current authors as a win-win situation where everyone involved can and should benefit. Shareholders of the company being acquired through a buyout receive a substantial premium for their shares that are purchased above market value. Employees of the company have an opportunity for greater career opportunities. Customers and the communities where the company is located benefit through the eventual growth of the company which translates into more and greater diversity of products for customers and additional employment opportunities and taxes to the communities. In addition, financial intermediaries ultimately benefit through the offering of junk bonds as a mode of debt financing. Junk bonds are high-risk and offer a higher than average return to investors.

Managers benefit since they gain control of the company and ultimately a share in the profits. The entrepreneur's benefits are similar to those of the manager with the added benefit that through buyout, the entrepreneur need not begin with only a concept and business plan in order to obtain financing.

The new owners of the company, the management of the company or an outside entrepreneur, enjoy several advantages when the company goes private. Among these is freedom from the extensive public disclosure and financial reports that come under close scrutiny of shareholders of public companies and often become the ammunition used in complaining to management about short-term earnings and profits. In the case of management buyout, the managers who now directly control the company are the best informed about the company and the resulting decisions should result in much better operations. Productivity increases also occur as restructuring increases efficiency of operations. Managers now have the additional motivational factor of sharing in company profits. Entrepreneurs in particular are pleased with the marketability of the company should a later decision be made to reenter the public traded sector through a stock offering.

Going private provides several tax advantages to both management and entrepreneurs. These include the buyer accounting for the acquisition as a purchase of assets, a procedure allowing the aggregate value of the assets to be increased from book value (cost less depreciation) to market value at the date of acquisition (usually a higher figure). This procedure permits a greater amount of depreciation, decreasing taxable income and tax liability.

BUYOUT RISKS

In spite of the attractiveness of the buyout option to both company management and entrepreneurs and the steadily increasing percentage of business acquisitions and startups that involve buyouts, there are serious risks to consider. Clemens P. Work and Manuel Schiffres comment that excessive debts, high interest rates, and the possibility of a recession could combine to burst the buyout bubble. Citing the purchase of Gibson Greeting Cards from RCA in 1982 and other buyouts that occurred in the first half of this decade, Work and Schiffres maintain that successful buyouts do not just happen but require aggressive management to produce profits and reduce debt.

THE NEW ENTREPRENEUR

Diane Cole, discussing the psychological side of the phenomenon of the new entrepreneur, quotes recent survey results that claim 38 percent of men and 50 percent of women to today's workforce want to start their own company. Cole notes that the principal creator of jobs in the American economy is the new entrepreneur who has started a new company or acquired one through buyout. She notes that in 1965 there were only 204,000 business startups compared to 700,000 in 1988.

Experts suggest a variety of reasons for the relentless pursuit of the new entrepreneur. Harry Levinson, president of Levinson Institute in Baltimore, says that the driving force is not greed but psychological compulsion. The entrepreneur is driven by an unresolved rivalry with his father and unconsciously strives to defeat him and escape from his control. Levinson notes that the entrepreneur will work only for himself and cannot tolerate authority.

Albert Shapiro, professor of management at Ohio State Graduate School of Business, points to the entrepreneur's striving for autonomy, independence, and self-reliance (an internal focus of control) as the primary motivating factor. This all-consuming drive that forces the entrepreneur onward stems from conscious feelings of deprivation and guilt stemming from broken family relationships that have occurred in the process, according to George Gilder, author of *The Spirit of Enterprise*. A. David Silver, in *The Entrepreneurial Life*, points to the fact that over half of the entrepreneurs were involved in a divorce along the road to success.

Levinson notes there are few female entrepreneurs. Survey results concur with Levinson's observations. Levinson believes that women are not driven by the same level of intensity. Historically, women have lacked both the role model and the capital needed to undertake such intensive approaches. Levinson suggests that raising a family and managing a household require timeless commitment and energy similar to that exhibited by entrepreneurial men and so suggests that women with the intensive drive seen in successful entrepreneurs may satisfy it through the demands her family places on her.

ATTRACTIVENESS OF BUYOUTS TO ENTREPRENEURS

New entrepreneurs employ a variety of creative ways to start and acquire companies. They have seen the opportunity for rapid gains that buyouts offer and many choose to use the buyouts as an additional approach to owning a business. Well-acquainted with risk taking, some entrepreneurs opt to use the E-LBO, acquiring an established business as opposed to the more traditional approach of founding a company.

In an E-LBO, the entrepreneur decides to buy out a company whose profits are known. While there may be considerable risk, it is not as great a risk factor as establishing a new company which obviously lacks any track record. In either case, financing is a major factor to be considered. Other entrepreneurs are discovering new products or businesses and are using creative approaches to provide products or services as well as seek the needed financing.

For example, Scott McNealy refused to believe that foreign competition had the workstation segment of the computer industry locked up and set out to develop an inexpensive, high-quality computer that used standard industry software. He founded Sun Microsystems Inc. He dealt with the Japanese and today has license agreements with Toshiba and Tokyo Electron Labs to sell Sun computers. The fastest-growing company in the workstation industry, Sun reported $1.8 billion in revenues in 1988.

Chemist George Rathmann, co-founder of Angen Inc., was not discouraged when established drug companies failed to show interest and provide the venture capital needed for the pharmaceuticals he developed and knew to be safe and effective. His development of a blood hormone attracted the attention of Keran, a Japanese brewery, who offered $12 million to build Rathmann's company. He accepted the offer.

Others have stumbled across opportunities because they saw a need for a product or service, or needed the product or service personally and developed a way to meet the need. Rob and Betty Pepper, operators of a fledgling toy store in Ormond Beach, Florida, discovered many customers seeking swing sets that they could assemble themselves. Unable to locate a supplier, the Peppers designed a build-your-own set, located a company in Taiwan to provide the materials, and took out a second mortgage on their home to finance Child Works Inc. The company broke even in 1987, made a profit in 1988, and has done so well that the Peppers closed the toy store to devote themselves full time to their company.

When Wendie Every could not find a suitable Christmas card for her husband's business, she designed one of her own. Impressed clients who received the cards asked Wendie to design cards for them. Taking on a partner in 1984, they formed We Create Ltd. and sold 15,000 cards in 1985. Business grew and in 1988 the company sold 350,000 cards with $325,000 in sales.

BUYOUT FINANCING

Entrepreneurs sometimes have problems convincing financial institutions to provide them with the capital necessary to begin a new business. Normally, however, these financial institutions are willing to help finance E-LBOs because the risk factor is much lower than financing a new venture. Leaders of financial institutions are aware of the fact that entrepreneurs are likely to be educated and knowledgeable about the field into which they are buying. Also, major investors are likely to be wealthy, reinforcing their success as entrepreneurs and reassuring the lender. An institutional lender feels safer about investing his institution's funds in an E-LBO when the entrepreneur himself is making a large contribution.

Another characteristic of institutional lenders is the long repayment period they are more than likely to provide. This is due to the confidence the lenders gain in E-LBOs. They do not feel a need to demand the money in a short period of time because the company is unlikely to have any great cash flow in the starting stages. At the same time, leveraged financiers earn more interest over the longer repayment period. Forstmann Little and Co., one of the major New York City investment firms, has financed buyouts such as Revlon, Dr. Pepper Co., and Allen-Bradley Co. In order to feel even safer about their investment, lending companies such as these often seek to secure loans with personal guarantees, especially when the amount is substantial.

It should be noted that these institutional lenders often charge a much lower interest rate to those in E-LBO transactions than nonentrepreneurial LBO investors. As previously stated, this is because of the confidence of a stable industry, established companies, and respected investors.

As we have seen, institutional lenders find it more profitable to invest in E-LBOs rather than new ventures. Knowing the history of the entrepreneur is an advantage to the lenders to ensure safety of their loaned funds. This is sort of a reciprocal agreement in which the lenders are confident in their investment in E-LBOs while the entrepreneurs receive a lower interest rate on their loans.

MANAGEMENT BUYOUTS

The first national conference on management buyouts (MBO), held at Nottingham University in early 1981, posed the question, "Management Buyouts—Corporate Trend for the 1980s?" From small beginnings prior to 1980, the buyout marketplace developed rapidly in the first half of the decade, so that in 1985 an estimated 229 buyouts took place, according to the Centre for Management Buyout Research. Today buyouts are an important feature of our economy. Having appeared on the corporate scene tentatively late in the 1970s, MBO has become, in less than a decade, a well-established means to transfer company ownership.

MISCONCEPTIONS

The national media and business theorists often paint the picture of a company ripe for takeover by either LBO, MBO, or ESOP as one that is teetering on the brink of failure and cash-poor. However, by surveying attitudes of managers involved in buyouts, it becomes apparent that financial difficulties are a factor most buyout parties seek to avoid. Rather, parties in search of buyout opportunities are seeking companies that show stable past profits and promising profit forecasts; little or no growth in a stable, mature industry; a strong and aggressive management team; and impressive current assets. Clearly in the case of buyouts,

Table 7.1
Frequency Distribution of Respondents

Question: The company I am working for was not doing
well before the buyout.

Respondents Choice	Frequency	
	Nos.	%
Total Agree:	13	28%
Total Disagree:	30	64%
Indifferent:	4	8%

business practices differ radically from business theory. Buyouts benefit both the company and the corporate manager and improve the activity of the board of directors regarding company operations and decision making.

MANAGEMENT'S PERCEPTION OF BUYOUTS

In order to determine management's perception of buyouts, a random sample was drawn from 45 companies that went private within the last five years. Of the 260 managers who were selected to complete the survey, 47 responded for a response rate of about 18 percent. Most of the questions used in the survey were drawn from statements made by managers in a variety of business articles.

A pilot study was performed (ten managers surveyed) to test the questionnaire. Subsequent to the pilot study, minor adjustments were made to the survey instrument.

The first question of the survey sought to determine how profitable the company was prior to the buyout. About 64 percent responded that the company was doing well before the buyout (see tab. 7.1). A common characteristic of buyout targets is an extremely successful past but a recent decline in profits. Such companies are the most attractive buyout targets. They rapidly improve their bottom line after buyout with an average value increase of 8.4 percent.

Buyouts occur because management knows their business. Managers have the inside information that tells them their company is worth more. While managers receive good salaries and benefits, they know a greater return—including a share of the profits—is possible through buyout. While there is great personal risk involved, there is also an opportunity for an equally great reward.

The second survey question asked respondents if they would have lost their jobs had the company not been taken private. An overwhelming 83 percent of the managers surveyed said they did not believe their

Table 7.2
Frequency Distribution of Respondents

Question: I certainly would have lost my job if the
            company did not go private.

Respondents Choice	Frequency	
	Nos.	%
Total Agree:	3	6%
Total Disagree:	39	83%
Indifferent:	5	11%

Table 7.3
Frequency Distribution of Respondents

Question: Our Board of Directors is actively involved
          in our strategic decision making.

Respondents Choice	Frequency	
	Nos.	%
Total Agree:	26	55%
Total Disagree:	11	23%
Indifferent:	10	22%

jobs were in jeopardy (see tab. 7.2). This again is a contradiction of current thought that financially troubled companies that are on the brink of being forced to cut management staff are the most likely buyout targets. It should be noted that following a buyout there may be management cuts because of the need to stretch dollars, reduce costs, and deal with the heavy debt burden. Recent studies indicate that what managers fear most is losing their jobs during the buyout.

The third survey question asked about involvement of the board of directors in strategic decision making. Once again, the commonly held view of corporate board involvement being minimal and more of a rubber stamp of CEO policy was not supported by survey data (see tab. 7.3). Boards are often seen as composed of personal friends and CEOs from other corporations who have been selected, not for their expertise but because of allegiance to the person at the helm of the corporation. While this may occur in public corporations, the survey demonstrated that this was not true of private companies that were recent buyout targets.

Survey results showed that 55 percent of respondents indicated a high level of board involvement in strategic decision making while only 23 percent indicated that their boards were not involved in this critical activity. Board members may rise to the task when they are involved in direct ownership rather than simply making decisions that affect the operation of the firm. Since the opportunity for success and profit is

Table 7.4
Frequency Distribution of Respondents

Question: In general, going private has been beneficial
to our company.

Respondents Choice	Frequency	
	Nos.	%
Total Agree:	34	72%
Total Disagree:	8	17%
Indifferent:	5	11%

Table 7.5
Frequency Distribution of Respondents

Question: I personally regret the company having been
taken private.

Respondents Choice	Frequency	
	Nos.	%
Total Agree:	7	15%
Total Disagree:	30	64%
Indifferent:	10	21%

greater after a buyout and the burden rests more directly on their shoulders, board members will assume greater responsibility for planning the future of the company.

Questions 4 and 5 in the survey were related. Question 4 asked managers if they saw going private as beneficial while question 5 asked if they regretted going private. Analysis showed that 72 percent believed going private was beneficial while 64 percent said they did not regret the change. Going private benefits both the company and its managers because of the opportunity for wealth in a relatively short period of time (see tabs. 7.4 and 7.5). In addition, the fear of being unable to meet the heavy interest and principal payments on the debt intensifies the manager's commitment to work. Following the buyout low-return segments of the company are usually unloaded, permitting operations to focus on the areas of the company with the strongest cash flow and highest rate of return. Going private removes the pressure of showing profitable quarterly earnings and permits implementing the best strategies for long-term profitability.

There is less bureaucracy after a buyout which leads to faster decision making than when board members act on behalf of behind-the-scenes stockholders. Employee compensation is more closely tied to performance following a buyout. Cash can be spent more carefully and pertinent information about the state of the company can be better communicated throughout the organization.

Table 7.6
Frequency Distribution of Respondents

Question: By going private, we have saved all or
          most employees.

Respondents Choice	Frequency	
	Nos.	%
Saved all employees jobs:	0	0%
Saved most employees jobs:	12	26%
Laid off some employees to keep costs down:	33	72%
Laid off some management to keep costs down:	16	35%
No Answer:	1	2%

Question 6 asked managers if taking the company private saved all
or most employee jobs. Results showed that cost-cutting moves resulted
in some employees losing their jobs while some managers were cut
following the buyout. None of the respondents said the company saved
all jobs following the buyout (see tab. 7.6). This is one of the few times
when survey results and national perception of buyout characteristics
matched. Theorists call for preserving most management jobs while
cutting line employees to revamp the company through cost reduction
in order to return it to a growth stage of the life-cycle.

The survey also provides a profile of the typical manager of a company
taken private through buyout as well as some information about buyout
targets. The results support the description of the new entrepreneur,
especially in regard to gender, age, and compensation level.

CONCLUSION

Restructuring has been taking place within many of America's large
corporations. Given such names as demassing and downsizing, this
restructuring has resulted in the loss of many jobs. Most companies
which move from public to private have lost employees and managers.
The survey shows that about 72 percent of those companies which responded have laid off some of their employees and about 35 percent
have laid off some of their managers. In the past two years close to a
half-million white-collar workers have left their jobs—some by way of
hefty separation incentives, some by dismissal.

Regardless of why restructuring and cutbacks are taking place, one
thing seems to be evident: "such cost-cutting programs are changing

Table 7.7
Profile of Buyout Targets

	Frequency	
A. Age of manager:	Nos.	%
Under 29	0	0%
30 - 39	2	4%
40 - 49	15	32%
50 - 59	24	51%
60 and over	6	13%
B. Sex of manager:	Nos.	%
Female	4	9%
Male	43	91%
C. Average annual income of manager:		
Under $39,999	0	0%
$40,000 - $59,999	2	4%
$60,000 - 79,999	2	4%
$80,000 - $99,999	6	13%
$100,000 and over	37	79%
D. People employed by company:		
Under 99	0	0%
100 - 299	9	20%
300 - 499	11	24%
500 and over	27	56%
E. Annual company sales for past fiscal year:		
Under $99,000	0	0%
$100,000-$499,999	1	2%
$500,000-$999,999	8	16%
$1,000,000-4,999,999	12	26%
$5,000,000 and over	26	56%
F. Type of business or industry company is involved in:		
Retail	19	40%
Manufacturing	15	32%
Industrial	3	6%
Communications	5	10%
Other	7	12%

the fabric of the American corporation."[1] Also such measures are threatening to destroy corporate loyalty and organizational commitment. For example, a survey conducted in 1986 of middle managers found that 65 percent of them regarded salaried employees as less loyal to their company as compared to ten years ago.[2]

The long-term effects of liquidating investments in human resources are unclear, but it seems that corporations may eventually pay a stiff price. Although there are employees who are not dismissed at the time of the restructuring, they are often demoralized and begin to wonder when their jobs will be terminated. This affects their feelings about the organization and their productivity.

NOTES

1. Bruce Nussbaum, "The End of Corporate Loyalty?" *Business Week* (August 4, 1986), pp. 42–45.
2. Ibid.

BIBLIOGRAPHY

Work, Clemens P., and Manuel Schiffres. "Leveraged Buyouts—Are They Growing Too Risky?" *U.S. News and World Report* (November 18, 1985): 49–52.
Cole, Diane. "The Entrepreneurial Self." *Psychology Today* (June 1989): 60–63.
Gilder, George. "New Breed of Innovator." *Success* (September 1988).
Harding, Susan D., Leon Hanouille, Joseph C. Rue, and Ara G. Volkan. "Why LBOs Are Popular." *Management Accounting* (December 1985): 51–56.
Jaffe, Charles A. "Success by Surprise." *Nation's Business* (September 1989): 30–32.
Kotkin, Joel. "What I Do in Private Is My Own Business." *INC* (November 1986): 66–81.
McComas, Maggie. "Life Isn't Easy." *Fortune* (December 9, 1985): 43–47.
Wyatt, Oscar S., Jr. "Acquisitions: Everyone Can and Should Benefit." *Industry Week* (September 30, 1985): 14.

8

CORPORATE GOVERNANCE AND THE RESTRUCTURING PROCESS

Today's board of directors is changing its role in large business. Most boards in the past were ineffective because the management controlled board members. Directors were usually chosen by the CEO with top management's influence. The CEO would typically select some of directors from top-level management (insiders) and the others from outside the organization who were normally friends. No one would dispute the CEO's decisions and whatever he had to say was the way it would be. Myles L. Mace's 1971 interviews with chief executives support this conclusion. For instance, he quotes one chief executive who said, "In selecting new outsider directors, I pick them very much like a trial jury." Another president said, "Don't be surprised or disappointed if you find that most outsider members are known to be no boat-rockers. . . . You certainly don't want anyone on your board who even slightly might be a challenge or question to your tenure."[1]

This was the way most boards were run and not until recently has anything been done to change it. Serving on a board of directors was once considered a prestigious position. Today's potential board members, concerned about liability, are turning down the invitation. The board of directors is liable to shareholders if the company is failing. If the board fails to act in the best interest of its shareholders, shareholders may sue. Even if the board only appears negligent, they may find themselves pulled into court by shareholders.

Figure 8.1
The Traditional BOD

A recent poll of one thousand companies by *Fortune* magazine showed that 86 percent of the firms polled combine the jobs of chairman, board of directors, and CEO into one.[2] According to Thomas H. Mitchell, appointing the chief executive officer or any other inside director as the chairman of the board of directors undermines the board's ability to exercise independent oversight of senior managers. In addition the board's ability to serve as guardian of stockholder interests in the system of corporate checks and balances is also jeopardized.[3]

THE EVOLUTION OF THE BOARD

The board over the years has changed dramatically, from being very simple to greatly complex. In the traditional model, (see Fig. 8.1), the stockholders would nominate and elect directors who were responsible for the operation of the business and accountable to the stockholders. This type of board was successful for many years, but today's boards are far different.

The structure of boards varies considerably, depending on the type and size of the business. In a company dominated by the owner-manager (sole proprietorship), the board is simply there to ratify the decisions already made by the owner-manager. Most directors are either relatives or those who have a special relationship with the owner-manager. This type of company is proprietorial because the power comes from the owner. The main problem is that one man cannot oversee the whole operation, especially with respect to external capital.

A second type of company is run by a family or second generation of the founders. There are generally a few relatives on the board; the rest of the members are top executives who rely on the company for their jobs. Board meetings are dominated by the chairman. There may be a meeting beforehand to discuss the agenda and agree on what will be discussed.

The third type of board is that of a large publicly owned company. This type of board is made up of a number of outside and inside directors. A problem with this type of board is that an outside director generally does not know enough about the company's operation.

Figure 8.2
Links Between Governance and Management

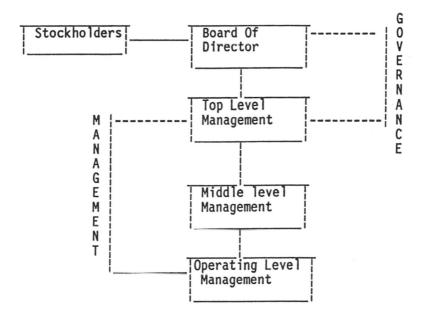

MANAGING AND GOVERNING

When individuals operate their own company, there is little cause to distinguish between governance and management. However, in large public companies, managing and governing roles are separated. The roles of the chief executive officer and the chairman of the board will be well defined with regard to who manages and who governs (see fig. 8.2).

The establishment of a legal entity with a large number of shareholders in today's economy requires a separation between owners and managers. The underlying assumption of such a separation is the appropriate allocation of corporate resources. Owners and managers might have a different interest in the existence of the corporation. Management is basically responsible for running the operation of a particular business. The classical management team is like a pyramid with a hierarchy of command.

Management focuses on how to run the entity efficiently and effectively through the traditional functions of planning, organizing, directing, and controlling. Management is also involved in the decision-making process concerning product design, procedures, financing, and product market. Ownership is concerned with the necessary capital and therefore has the right to protect its property.

Corporate governance is not the responsibility of management but that of the board. The board is responsible for the strategic direction in which the company plans to go. The board supervises and oversees top management, and is accountable to the stockholders. The board is also different from the top management because there is no hierarchy of command; all directors are equally responsible in regards to corporate governance.

Although there is a distinction between management and the board, they regularly interact in the making or confirmation of major decisions. Furthermore, some top-level management might be on the board. When top-level managers are on the board they must make a distinction between their duties as employees and their duties as board members.

BOARD LIABILITY

Although the CEO plays a major role in the decisions that the board of directors makes, directors must realize that their job is not to satisfy the CEO but to satisfy the stockholders. Benjamin M. Rosen, chairman of Compaq Computer, states the boards should be a check on management: "I think that the owners of the company should be represented by the directors. That has ceased to happen at lots of companies where Management dominates the Board."[4] Harold S. Geneen, former chief of ITT, states: "The role of the Board is not to be a contender against Management. Its role is to help Management."[5] The board needs to be aware at all times what is going on inside the company which it represents.

Roles and expectations differ among board members; the most influential members usually get their way. Board members must be aware of how the company is being run and take a stand on what they believe. Members must recognize what constitutes good performance, have an awareness of their firm's performance level, be familiar with the severity of particular company problems, and know top management's ability to alter the firm's performance. If the board believes that the firm is not performing up to expectations and that it is top management's responsibility, then the board should dismiss the CEO. Yet mistakes can be made. "The mere presence of dissenting expectations and attributions within the Board increases the likelihood for dismissal."[6] A good example of the board not being aware of what was going on is the case of Allegheny International. CEO Robert J. Buckley was helping himself generously to corporate money. In 1984 he paid himself $1 million in compensation when the company's total earnings were only $14.9 million. He also spent millions more without the board knowing anything. In 1986, his crime became public and the stockholders sued the board for "waste of corporate assets and grossly improper business decisions."[7] Many well-known people, including Alexander Haig and Anthony O'Reilly, were on the board. This case shows that, even with an influential board, a company may be poorly run.

The board's allegiances and values are very important to how an organization is run and how long the CEO serves. Board members serve for different reasons (wealth maximization, steady director's fees, status, reputation, comradery) and their decisions are based on this fact. A board member who is a major shareholder will have different ideas than a member who is hand-picked by the CEO. A problem when deciding to hire or fire a CEO is whether the board members are looking out for themselves or the stockholders. In either case, there will be many debates.

A major problem that many companies face is that the CEO and chairman of the board are one and the same. The majority of analysts believe that this should be a dual function. In this case, the CEO/chairman chooses the members of the board and also sets the agenda at meetings. Murray Weidenbaum, former chairman of Reagan's Counsel of Economic Advisors and a director of three companies, states, "It's awkward to put it mildly, to have the same person preside over the governing process and present the main proposals."[8] Although the CEO/chairman are still the same in many companies, big companies such as Compaq, RJR Nabisco, Motorola, and Texaco have successfully split the jobs.

Today's legal environment is changing the relationship between board directors and stockholders. Federal law is vague when it comes to director's responsibilities. Some states are going further by making directors act with loyalty, honesty, and care. The law has been changing since the 1960s when shareholder litigation exploded. In 1985 many large corporations were terrified because of a ruling on a shareholder suit against ten board members of Trans Union Corporation. The court ruled that the directors were "negligent when they agreed to sell the Railcan-Leasing Company to the Pritzker Family's Mommon Group in a hasty, two hour meeting dominated by the CEO."[9] The board members did not pay a cent because an insurer paid $10 million of the settlement and the Pritzkers came up with the rest. Although the board members did not pay anything, people started to worry about serving on a board, since they could face personal bankruptcy. Today many top executives and others will not serve on boards for fear they will be sued. The insurance premiums for members are astronomical and many companies are reducing the size of their boards. A 1989 survey conducted by the author showed that about 96 percent of the companies who went private have a smaller board than before. Some say that this whole incident was blown out of proportion and that there were only a few actual cases when the board was sued. In either case a board should be held accountable for their actions if the stockholders are not notified and if decisions are made that are not in the stockholders' best interest.

THE ROLE OF THE BOARD OF DIRECTORS

Two principles have been applied by the courts in dealing with the responsibility a board has in the event of a takeover: "When the board's decision has taken on the appropriate defensive tactic, it must be reasonable in relation to the perceived threat to the corporation."[10] It is assumed that the board will always act in the best interest of the corporation. Another principle is that once the board takes action toward selling the company or approving a change of control of the company, its duty changes. The initial duty for the best interest of its shareholders has changed. Its main focus becomes treating all bidders fairly and maximizing prices.

Whenever a buyout takes place, the board and shareholders have special duties. The board has a responsibility to its shareholders and other groups such as employees, creditors, customers, suppliers, and local communities. The board should oppose a buyout if the majority of shareholders are not supportive.

It is obvious that the board's duty is to protect shareholders, but it is often unclear whether the board *adequately* protects them. In some circumstances, it will be impossible to convince shareholders of the full value of the shares. When inside knowledge is critical, this places the board in a very critical situation. Most of the time, the board agrees on such deals when faced with an anticipated buyout.

When management considers a buyout, the board members must treat shareholders, employees, creditors, customers, suppliers, and local communities fairly. Stakeholders can claim the right to object to a management buyout on the grounds that they have made a larger investment than persons who trade the shares on a daily basis. The corporate charter, granted by the state, focuses on the obligation of the board to act in a way that recognizes public interest. Therefore, the board is responsible for both voting and nonvoting groups.

THE LBO TRANSACTION

The LBO transaction goes through the following steps:

Figure 8.3
The LBO Transaction

PURCHASING GROUP	TYPE OF BUYOUT	FINANCIAL SUPPORT	CORPORATE GOVERNANCE	NEW COMPANY
MANAGEMENT	MBO	COMMERCIAL BANKS, INSURANCE CO. SPECIALIST FINANCE	STOCKHOLDERS	NEW COMPANY EMERGED
INVESTORS	LBO	COMPANIES PENSION FUNDS SMALL BUSINESS	BOARD OF DIRECTORS	
EMPLOYEE	ESOP	INVESTMENT CO. VENTURE CAPITALIST OTHERS	MANAGEMENT	
COMBINATION	LBO		EMPLOYEES	

1. The management, or outside investors, or employees of the corporation in the ESOP, or several of these groups together present a proposal to the acquiring company.

2. This proposal must be supported by a financial package, including the name of the bank(s), insurance companies, pension plans, and the like which are supporting the proposal with financial details. The financial package represents the agreement between the parties who consent to finance the LBO.

3. This deal is usually presented to the board of directors (BOD) of the acquiring company. The BOD is the stockholders' representative. If the BOD feels that the deal is an attractive one then it will present it to the stockholders for approval.

4. When the stockholders accept the deal, especially if the offer price is higher than the market price, then the stockholders sell their stock to the purchasing group at the agreed-upon price.

5. The final stage after the stockholders' agreement is the formation of a new business entity. (These stages are presented in fig. 8.3).

6. Sometimes employees enter into the picture by demanding an agreement with the new purchaser, especially if they were unionized.

NOTES

1. Myles L. Mace, *Director: Myth and Reality* (Boston: Harvard College, 1971), pp. 78–79.

2. Thomas H. Mitchell, "Chairman and Chief Executive Officer: A Conflict of Rules?" *Canadian Business Review* (Spring 1988): 30.

3. Ibid.

4. Charles C. Krusekopf, "Pushing Corporate Boards to Be Better," *Fortune* (July 18, 1988).

5. Ibid.

6. James W. Fredrickson, Donald C. Hambreck, and Sara Baumron,"A Model of CEO Dismissal," *Academy of Management Review* (September 1988).

7. Krusekopf, "Pushing Corporate Boards."

8. Ibid.

9. Fredrickson, Hambreck, and Baumron, "Model of CEO Dismissal."

10. Ajit Singh, *Takeover* (Cambridge University Press, 1971), pp. 20–22.

BIBLIOGRAPHY

Andrews, Kenneth R. "Rigid Rules Will Not Make a Good Board," *Harvard Business Review* (November–December 1982): 34–35.

Business Roundtable. *The Role and Composition of the Board of Directors of the Large Publicly Owned Corporations* (New York, 1978), p. 15.

Lewin, Tamar. "The Corporate Reform Furor." *New York Times* (June 10, 1982): D–1.

Lewis, Ralph F. "What Should Audit Committees Do?" *Harvard Business Review* (May–June 1978): 22, 26, 172, 174.

Mathes, Sorrell M. "The Smaller Company's Board of Directors." (Conference Board, 1967).

Tricker, R. I. "Improving the Board's Effectiveness." *Journal of General Management* (Spring 1987): 460.

9

INTERNATIONAL BUYOUTS

THE DEVELOPMENT OF INTERNATIONAL BUYOUTS

International buyouts typically appeal to the prosperous firm which has had prior international experience and which seeks to obtain a business relative to the firm's core operations. Few companies in the initial stages of international operations are willing to invest a large portion of their resources in foreign operations. A major motive for seeking an acquisition is that a potential investor may find it difficult to transfer resources to an existing foreign operation or to locally acquire resources for a proposed foreign facility. In 1960, many corporations decided to merge or acquire other businesses that were not in the same industry. This strategy was mainly to reduce the risk of business failure by spreading revenues over diverse groupings of the business entity. According to George Steiner (1975), only a small portion of such merging firms were successful.

A reverse strategy dominated the recessionary period of the 1970s that prompted the sale of many companies, divisions, and subsidiaries. Merged corporations, faced with increased competition in the market-place, were forced to either liquidate subsidiaries to stay competitive or to sell successful subsidiaries to offset large losses within the corporation's core operation.

This type of strategy continues today as corporations attempt to remain competitive and use their resources as efficiently as possible. Management continuously assesses the corporate environment and attempts to modify strategy in response to changes in the environment. The result is that many companies are open to potential investors seeking new financial opportunities and challenges.

Inflation increases buyouts due to the fact that inflation benefits debtors. LBOs sharply increased from $636 million in 1979 to $10.8 billion in 1984.[1] Mergers, acquisitions, and LBOs in 1978 accounted for less than 5 percent of the profits of Wall Street brokerage houses; in 1988, these activities were estimated to be 50 percent of the profits.[2]

INTERNATIONAL LBOs

The desire for greater growth in a shorter time period is another factor which entices one firm to seek to acquire another firm. Oligopoly considerations can also influence acquisition activity within highly concentrated industries. Yet another reason for one firm wanting to acquire another is that companies from countries with relatively low-cost capital will value earnings from foreign operations above domestic earnings. The lower capital costs reflect lower monetary discount rates which result in higher net value of foreign earnings. Finally, a firm may save money if it buys an existing firm that provides the company with a brand identification and reputation which could be very costly to develop in a foreign country. A good example of this is the Ford–GM battle over a bigger market share in Europe. Ford finally agreed to pay more than $2.5 billion to acquire Jaguar, the leading British luxury-auto company. Some analysts think that Ford did not necessarily make a wise investment. Bob Barber, an auto-industry analyst at James Capel & Co. in London, was quoted as saying, "I don't believe the company is worth anywhere near what [Ford] has paid for it."[3]

When compared with the development of a subsidiary in a foreign country, buyouts reduce costs and risks as well as provide quicker results. In addition, buyouts provide a way of becoming a part of a foreign market without adding production capacity to that market.

One of the most important facets of international acquisition is the management style which the acquiring firm practices. If the firm believes that it can assume a passive role, expecting the subsidiary to basically take care of itself, financial troubles will surface. That is because the incentives for the affiliate to match its former performance are reduced. Management may no longer have the same incentive to perform under the new arrangement as it did when the company was more independent. Problems also arise when the management team is replaced or when the foreign firm attempts to require existing personnel, facilities, and systems to conform to global standards. In such cases acquisition can be more time-consuming, costly, and problematic than developing a new operation.

INTERNATIONAL BUYOUTS: THE UNITED STATES, GREAT BRITAIN, AND FRANCE

Compared to the United States, buyouts in Great Britain were generally smaller until the mid-1980s. In 1980, the number of completed buyouts reached one hundred and by the mid-1980s was running at somewhere around two hundred per year. As a means of securing their own future employment and with the prospect of a longer-term capital gain, managers have become willing buyers since 1979. Due to the rehabilitation of the concept of entrepreneurship within the British economy, more individuals are prepared to strike out in business on their own. The government has also offered positive encouragement.

The distinguishing features of venture capital are that it involves some equity participation, is generally a long-term investment decision, and includes some form of active relationship between the venture capitalist and the entrepreneurial management teams. It is generally aimed at young companies, although it may also come into capital reconstructions and development finance. Within the venture capital industry, the majority of investments in buyouts have come from those venture organizations which are part of major financial institutions. The latest development in the buyout marketplace, as far as funding is concerned, was the emergence in 1985 of specialist funds earmarked for buyouts. During the 1980s very few entries in the *Investors Chronicle* listed buyouts; however, by 1985 buyout was a preferred area of interest.

In Great Britain, the buyouts that have taken place so far can be divided into four major categories: buyouts of independent companies which are in receivership; buyouts from parent companies in receivership; buyouts from parent companies by way of conventional divestment; and buyouts on the retirement of the previous owners. The retirement category can be further subdivided into those which arise from the genuine retirement of the owner of a family firm and those where it is simply a decision of the current owners to withdraw from owning a particular firm.[4] The divestment category accounts for the majority of buyouts and contradicts a still commonly held belief that buyouts are usually from receiverships and are exclusively the product of a recession.

The British marketplace reflects many of the developments that have taken place in the United States. Management buyouts have been part of the corporate scene in the United States since the early 1970s and have been a variant of the leveraged buyout concept which has enabled many companies in the United States to go private. The British marketplace has developed quite rapidly since 1980, and trends are already emerging which suggest that there will be further growth in terms of both the number of deals and the total value of the market. Buyout growth in the United States offers useful parallels and a good indication of how buyouts develop.

Although many owners and managers have asked themselves the question, "Why buy out?" and have found convincing answers, nevertheless there remain many for whom management buyouts have not been adopted as a tool of strategy. Buying out, like any transaction, requires a willing seller and a willing purchaser. The perspectives of the seller and the purchaser may be quite different, and will affect whether a buyout takes place and the form it takes.[5]

Great Britain is experiencing a rise in LBOs[6]: 124 buyouts worth a total of $100 million were arranged, but they still remain far behind the United States in total monetary amount. One of the largest buyouts Great Britain has experienced concerns Stone-Platt Industries. When the company went under, some divisions were sold to its managers; these divisions experienced higher profits than prior to the buyout. For example, its electrical division was sold for $15 million to managers led by Robin Travener, chief executive of the Stone-Platt group. This division made a $4.3-million profit before interest and tax in 1980. The finances for this buyout came from the manager, banks, pension funds, insurance companies, and specialist finance companies.[7]

Another major buyout in Britain was the divestment by Thorn EMI. The primary objective of the divestment by this conglomerate was to raise operating profit, which had shrunk 9 percent the previous year to $171.7 million ($216 million). Sales rose 14 percent $3.2 billion for the year until March 1985. The conglomerate's plan was to reduce the company to four product groups, rather than seven, so that efforts to increase profitability could be more focused. Three groups were divested. The major goal of this buyout was to reduce the risk of the three divested groups, while increasing the profitability of the remaining four.

The French government is lowering taxes in order to promote LBOs. A major problem, however, has been identified by Compagnie Financiere de Suez and the Paribas group, the two major French financial groups. Under present French law it is difficult for managers to set up a company of their own, with outside backing, so they can buy the firm they work for. New owners are seeking new laws which would allow them to use tax writeoffs. The groups who seem to be benefiting most from the LBOs in France are foreign-owned subsidiaries and family-owned firms, due to the government's new emphasis on entrepreneurship and small business.[8]

A major LBO took place in Canada in 1972, which in turn, has inspired others. CIP, Inc., a pulp and paper manufacturer, was bought out with a major part of the $13.5-million financial backing coming from the provincial government which contributed $4.4 million in grants and $6 million in loans; private investors contributed $200,000; the employees contributed $425,000; and the remaining $2.5 million came from preferred shares. The closing of CIP would have left over 700 laborers unemployed, but the new company, Tembec, has been very successful since the buyout.[9]

THE PROBLEM WITH LBOs

LBOs free companies from scrutinizing stockholders, let them escape from takeover bids, and allow them to concentrate on growth. However, these advantages are not without financial risks.

One such risk is a possible economic downturn. If the company's core business fluctuates with the economy, a subsequent recession would severely retard the company's earnings, thereby making it difficult to meet debt obligations. Another risk is a rise in interest rates not anticipated at the time of the buyout. When the market rate increases, an increase in the company's interest obligations over the original terms of the loan will also occur.[10] A company which is barely meeting its debt obligations may have some problems paying the increased interest payments. A final risk deals with legal matters. Shareholders who are opposed to the buyout may take the buyers to court if they feel they are being treated unjustly. For this reason, the buyers must make sure they are careful during the buyout process.

While LBOs are supported by many, they also have their share of critics. One criticism is that LBOs are not the noble endeavors that they might seem to be. They do not create jobs (often there is a "house cleaning"); they do not increase productivity; and often they do not help the company compete in the business world.

Another criticism is that the threat of LBOs encourages bad business practices. A typical LBO target is not a company in trouble, but a company which has a large amount of assets, low debt, and relatively consistent profits. Therefore, a company might elect to increase dividends or bonuses instead of upgrading factories, simply to avoid a takeover attempt. In the end all this will do is hurt the competitiveness of the business.

Finally, LBOs diminish the entrepreneurial spirit, turning the search for creative methods of business into a big-money game. Instead of developing new companies and practices, raiders strive for large amounts of money to take over already existing companies. Again, business is the one hurt in the end.[11]

CONCLUSION

We have seen that going private is not only a domestic phenomenon but also an international one. As long as a great profit motive is involved when the company goes private again, many managers and investors will continue to take the opportunity. We believe that many people are willing to invest in buyouts, since there have been very few failures. The number of buyouts will doubtless continue to grow. An issue that might be raised is whether the large debt taken on by these companies will help or hinder the economy in the long run.

When deciding which type of international business a firm should adopt, several factors must be taken into account. These include the legal environment, cost, experience, competition, risk control, and the nature of the assets. After taking these factors into consideration, the choice among licensing, joint ventures, and wholly owned subsidiaries can be structured within a portfolio perspective.

Even though it is difficult to accurately assess the question at this time because buyouts are a relatively new phenomenon, buyouts will probably help the national economy more than they will hinder it. Buyouts will probably stimulate the economy, encourage the spirit of being an entrepreneur, and circulate money. They will also hinder the economy through the loss of jobs, through pressure put on employees and managers to be more efficient, and through the stress on those who want to double their money in a short time period. The last word on LBOs has not been said by any means, but it will be interesting to see the trend that buyouts take when the economy changes in the future.

NOTES

1. Ellyn E. Spragins, "Leveraged Buyouts Aren't Just for Daredevils Anymore," *Business Week* (August 11, 1986): 50.

2. Robert B. Reich, "Leveraged Buyouts: America Pays the Price," *New York Times* (January 29, 1989): 32–40.

3. Joann S. Lublin and Craig Forman, "Ford Snares Jaguar, but $2.5 Billion Is High Price for Prestige," *Wall Street Journal* (November 3, 1989): 1.

4. John Coyne, *Management Buyouts* (Croomhelm, 1985), pp. 15–28.

5. Ibid., p. 8.

6. Coyne, *Management Buyouts*, p. 29; Susan D. Harding, Leon Hanouille, Joseph C. Rue, and Ara G. Volkan, "Why LBOs Are Popular," *Management Accounting* (December 1985): 51–52.

7. Rogene A. Bucholz, *Business Environment and Public Policy: Implications for*

Management and Strategy Formulation, 2d ed. (Englewood Cliffs, N.J.: Prentice-Hall, 1986), p. 247.

8. John Greenwald, "The Popular Game of Going Private," *Time* (November 4, 1985): 54.

9. Spragins, "Leveraged Buyouts Aren't Just for Daredevils Anymore", p. 50.

10. Zachary Schiller, "Uniroyal: The Road from Giant to Corporate Shell," *Business Week* (July 14, 1986): 29.

11. Harding, Hanouille, Rue, and Volkan, "Why LBOs Are Popular," p. 52.

10

EMPLOYEE STOCK OWNERSHIP PROGRAMS

A motivated employee is one who is personally responsible for his or her work and knows that it is in his or her own best interest to be more productive. One way to increase productivity is to offer employees part of the company. This can be accomplished by providing the employee with the option of buying company stock at a certain discount. Personal gain is thereby directly linked to performance in the company.

THE IMPORTANCE OF ESOPs

In the early part of this century, laborers had few rights, poor working conditions, and poor pay. Often workers were fired for attempts to form unions. Management had the advantage. The Wagner Act of 1935 made collective bargaining compulsory if a majority of the employees agreed to form a union.

The work environment improved for many workers after government legislation. In the 1960s and 1970s labor and management parties were often openly hostile toward each other when they bargained for a collective agreement. Labor mistrusted management because they felt they were not receiving a fair share of the profits. Mistrust deepened when management started shutting down plants and moving rather than reinvesting in existing facilities. From the manager's perspective, organized labor decreased productivity with restrictions such as extremely detailed job descriptions and union protection against firing.

If the United States is to be productive in the future, changes must be made in the management style of many businesses. International competition is becoming more difficult due to the restrictive trade tariffs imposed by certain international industrial areas like Japan and the European Common Market. Cooperation is needed within U.S. organizations if they intend to survive. More can be accomplished through cooperative interaction than through self-defeating internal struggles. Cooperation between labor and management is desperately needed. Cooperation may be improved through the formation of participative corporate government. One possible solution may be employee stock ownership programs (ESOPs).

ESOPs have been put in place in an ever-growing number of companies in recent years. Ever since 1974, when Congress enacted the first of a series of tax measures designed to encourage employee stock ownership plans, the number of employee-owned (or partially owned) companies has grown from about 1,600 to 8,100, and the number of employees owning stock has jumped from 250,000 to more than 8,000,000.[1]

THE PRODUCTIVITY ISSUE

Are employee stock option plans an effective method of increasing worker productivity? Is it possible that the share option plans only motivate those who are already motivated? Some employees already accept the role of company stakeholders and have positive feelings toward the company and their jobs. Could stock options bring about the same feelings in those people not yet motivated? What other forces influence an employee to place his or her financial future in a company? In some share option schemes, a pension plan is foregone in lieu of a stock ownership plan. Although setting up employee stock ownership plans has great benefits for the employer, it also poses great risks for the employee. How can a company prevent an employee from losing his entire life's work by entering into a stock option plan which provided for his pension, but becomes useless when the company goes broke? One may wonder if such a great risk is worth the possible rewards.

Phillip Dewe, Stephen Dunn, and Ray Richardson examined a savings-linked option in which eligible workers would be allowed to purchase shares of the company's stock at lower-than-market prices.[2] Setting aside a portion of his or her earnings for a five-to-seven-year period, the employee would have two options: to buy shares of the company stock at 10 percent below the current price of the stock, or to take the money.

Their study found that only 69 percent of the workers recognized their role as stakeholders and their right to own a piece of the company. The overall sentiment of the employees was that the program was a good way to save money. Those who did not want to join the ESOP worried about the payments and believed that the stock option tied them to the firm in such a way that they had no control over the company's stock price.

Those who do not recognize their role as stakeholder are those who do not feel secure enough to give the firm 100 percent. Therefore, they will not accept the option to be an actual owner. On the other hand, those who seem to recognize their role as stakeholder are motivated and feel secure in their position in the company. The opportunity to increase financial resources by participating in company ownership increases productivity motivation too.[3]

Ralph E. Drtina and Marshall R. Gunsel discuss the high risks that employees face by participating in stock option plans.[4] In 1974, the Employee Retirement Income Security Act established ESOPs. This act was intended to enable the employee to have a stake in the company he worked for. The act allowed the employee to share the wealth from the profits of the company along with regular salary payments. The employee's stake in the plan is primarily invested in the company's stock.

Generally more than 50 percent of the stock option is invested in the company's stock. This increases risk due to dependence upon one stock, though some of the funds are invested in other stocks. If the company's stock is destroyed, the employee has lost half of what he has worked for in one fell swoop. There are, however, some benefits for the employee under this program. The potential rewards are great. Owning stock in the corporation lets an employee exercise his or her role as stakeholder and also provides the feeling of being a part of the company. The employee gains a sense of personal control over his or her own economic future. The benefits for the employer seem to be much greater in this situation. Contributions to the plan are tax-deductible for the corporation. In this case, the employer either puts stock or the cash to purchase stock into a trust which is then credited to the employees. When an employee retires or leaves the company, he will receive the benefits from the plan.

At this point in the discussion, the difference between leveraged ESOPs and nonleveraged ESOPs must be clarified. A nonleveraged ESOP is set up in the form discussed so far in this chapter. A leveraged ESOP is different in that it allows the company to borrow the money to contribute to the plan. The company then puts the money into the ESOP which in turn pays the lender. So in essence the company pays off the loan in *pretax dollars*. The company also receives a tax-free rollover on stock contributed to the account. There is also a 50 percent interest exclusion for ESOP loans, and in 1986 the Tax Reform Act gave new incentives: a 50 percent exclusion on estate taxes when stock is sold to an ESOP, the deductibility of dividends on ESOP accounts used to pay a loan, accelerated deductions for corporate borrowing under leveraged plans, and a 50 percent income exclusion for mutual funds lending to ESOPs.[5]

There are disadvantages to the leveraged ESOP. When the ESOP purchases new issue stock for its plan, it will devaluate the stock of its shareholders unless the company generates the needed profits and growth to compensate for the new debt. Furthermore, the company still faces the problem of raising funds to buy out an employee when he or she leaves or retires. These risks are of great concern to the company, but such risks may have far greater effects on the employee. If the company does go bankrupt, the money is essentially gone. The company has already had use of the money; the employee has not. The rewards of his work and of his efforts have evaporated before his very eyes.

Rath Packing Company gave its employees a 60 percent stake in Rath in return for wage concessions. Even though this highly motivated the workers, Rath still failed. This left the employees with worthless Rath stock; their future economic security had disappeared. This was not a fair exchange. This problem could have been prevented by spreading the money out in other investments. About 80 percent of the current ESOPs have 75 percent invested in their own companies' stock, putting employees at great risk. One possible solution would be to invest 51 percent of the funds in the employee's company's stock and the remaining 49 percent in different, stable investments. This will cause decreased tax savings, increased transaction costs, and decreased motivation in employees. If employee motivation is not as great, the company will lose the growth it could obtain if the ESOP was more concentrated in the company stock. Other alternatives could be mutual funds, increased employee contributions, diversification of benefit packages, "floor plan" programs (having a bottom line for how much an employee can lose), and "hedging" programs (buying a stock whose value will definitely increase if the employee's company's stock value decreases).

According to Drtina and Gunsel, floor plan and hedging stock options ensure that the employee is treated fairly as an owner. With this in mind, it shows that the employee owner is not exercising his or her full power of decision making in the areas of corporate planning or budgeting. The final objective is to motivate the employee.[6]

The protected stock option seems to be a step in the right direction. There are several other facets to these benefit packages. Anup Agrawal and Gershon N. Mandelker maintain that the market will provide the required incentives for management.[7] This means that a successful and competitive company will have a highly compensated management. But other individuals believe that stock holdings and stock options are better incentives for those in management positions.

Agrawal and Mandelker conclude that stock option plans motivate some employees, but definitely motivate managers. Employees may not accept their governing role as stockholders, and the board and the management personnel may actually prefer to keep it that way. Dewe, Dunn, and Richardson found that only 69 percent of employees recognize their role as stakeholders. This fact may prevent the other 31 percent of workers from being motivated. They have little interest in the company let alone interest in owning part of it. On the other hand, the 69 percent already recognized their role as stakeholders and felt positive toward a role as owners.[8]

It is very difficult to have motivated employees when they feel that they are not truly involved in the company. The American worker generally accepts the role of stakeholder in name only for the possible financial benefits, but will not exercise his rights in strategic planning and budgeting as an owner.[9]

There may be basic ideological differences in employees around the globe. American employees trust the company with decisions that affect their future as long as a possible economic reward exists. Unfortunately, what happens to the trust placed in the board of directors and top management constitutes misuse and abuse. Examples of misuse of decision making are the pollution, corruption, and coercion which are largely ignored by American workers as long as they benefit financially from short-term actions. The British have dealt with the effects of industrial abuse on the environment before. One must not forget the smog that enveloped areas of Great Britain at the time of the advent of the coal-/wood-burning steam engine. Conditions were so critical that many British citizens believed the end of the world was approaching. Although the United States has been affected to a great extent by air pollution, it is still a relatively new problem to be corrected by the U.S. government via air regulation standards.

European employees recognize that they are representative of their society as a whole. Although U.S. employees will accept the role of profitable owner, the role of responsible steward is largely dismissed— the only exception being during the recent recession when large numbers of employees were left unemployed due to massive plant closings. Workers need to recognize their responsibility to society and their employer. And in turn the employer must recognize his responsibilities to the environment and to his employees.

THE ESOP PROCESS

Any system or process is bound to have flaws. But ESOPs have resulted in some very positive results once put in place. Employee stock ownership plans may allow for a complete buyout of a company by the employees or may operate in the form of profit sharing or a retirement plan for employees.

How are ESOPs used in practice to achieve results for the company and the employee? In an ESOP, a company can establish a trust fund. The employee stock ownership trust borrows money from banks or insurance companies. The company then makes contributions to the trust fund. The contributions are given in the form of either new issues of its own stock or cash to buy stock. Alternatively, the ESOP can borrow money to buy new or existing shares, with the company then making contributions to the ESOP to enable it to repay the loan. The ESOP can own anywhere from one to 100 percent of a company. The stock in the trust fund is then allocated to individual employee accounts.[10]

Who is eligible for stock and how much can they receive? The details will vary from company to company, but generally all employees over twenty-one years of age with more than one year of service can participate. Employees covered by a collective bargaining agreement can be excluded (provided the company bargains in good faith with them about this issue).[11]

Shares of stock are usually distributed based on the relative pay of each employee or based on seniority. An employee's shares will accumulate until he or she separates or retires from the company. When an employee leaves, he or she receives stock and the right to require the company to buy it back at its fair market value. Allocated shares can be sold, but only to employee stock ownership trust and not in the open market.[12]

This system of employee ownership helps the employee prepare financially for retirement. According to a 1985 National Center for Employee Ownership study, the typical employee in the typical ESOP accumulated $31,000 in stock after just ten years and $210,000 over twenty years.[13]

The typical ESOP allows employees 10 to 40 percent of the shares in their company. At least one-third of all plans will eventually afford workers the chance to acquire a controlling interest.[14]

Besides the financial benefits the employees receive there are benefits for the company too. Tax measures beginning in 1974 and continuing through the 1986 tax reform provide some good incentives. Today an ESOP can borrow money for such things as capital improvements. The company then makes tax-deductible contributions to the ESOP to repay the loan. In effect they are deducting both principal and interest, not just interest. Banks are encouraged to loan ESOP money. Lenders can deduct 50 percent of the interest income received on the ESOP loan. In practice, lenders are then passing part of this benefit to the company by lowering loan rates 10 to 20 percent.[15]

Financial incentives for the employees and the company are valid reasons to consider implementing an employee stock option plan, but there is by far much more depth to the ESOP concept. Employees receive more compensation for the work they do while increasing their own productivity in the company. The U.S. system of capitalism has an underlying message that says people will take better care of something if they own it rather than simply use it.

A volunteer worker in the inner city of Philadelphia brought up this ownership responsibility concept a few years ago when houses and apartments were accidentally destroyed by fire when the mayor tried to smoke out terrorist criminals in the community. The government rebuilt the area. Many of the residents were on welfare and did not own these buildings or their prior homes. These new buildings were well-designed, modern homes. The volunteer worker pointed out that as nice as these buildings were, within a year the area would look like a slum again because people simply did not appreciate what was given to them. On the other side ownership of a home does not guarantee good stewardship but in many cases it does give added incentive to take care of the lawn or the appearance of the home.

THE ESOP VERSUS THE TRADITIONAL MODEL

If owner responsibility is a sound theory, then companies that have partial or complete ownership should be more productive, grow faster, and be more profitable than traditional companies. In the traditional model stock is held by investors outside of the company. These outside investors are generally concerned only about the rate of return they are going to receive on their investment and not about how many families depend on the company for a living.

In a 1986 study, Corey Rosen and Michael Quarry found evidence to support this view. The study focused on forty-five companies that had ESOPs. Data for each company during the five years before it instituted the ESOP and then five years after were examined.

Rosen and Quarry chose at least five companies without ESOPs for each of the forty-five companies with ESOPs; as a result 238 companies were used for comparison. These companies were comparable to the ESOP companies in terms of business line, company size, and where possible, location. The study used data on sales and employment growth. Profit figures were not used because untarnished profit statements were unavailable.

The results showed that during the five years before instituting an ESOP, the 45 companies had, on average, grown moderately faster than the 238 comparison companies. Annual employment growth was 1.21 percent faster and sales growth was 1.89 percent faster. However, during the five years after these companies instituted ESOPs, their annual employment growth outstripped that of the comparison companies by 5.05 percent, while sales growth was 5.4 percent faster. Moreover, 73 percent of the ESOP companies in the sample significantly improved their performance after they set up their plans.[16]

EVALUATION

In retrospect, it appears that employees are motivated by stock options. We have discussed the risk involved with these stock options in the form of pension plans. This risk could be minimized by a more diverse investment practice. Yet management is not only motivated by stock options, but is also protected from their failure.[17]

When the general employee is left out in the cold because the stock price drops, the manager is offered a variety of safety nets. The previous agreement may be nullified and the option reorganized at the lower stock price, share for share. A "Godzilla grant" gives the executive the option of keeping the shares at the price at market; he then gets a large number of shares at the new lower strike price. The issue here is the manager's refusal to accept his or her stakeholder role. Rather than sacrifice any temporary lapse of remuneration for the company, the stockholders, or the employee, the manager wants his or her economic benefit restored immediately. Although the representative of the stockholders, the board, is informed, stockholders are not. Is the board really representing stockholders when it implements a plan that will decrease stockholder equity? Yet in general employees in this country do have a say in at least some of the board and managerial decisions.

Stock ownership plans for employees have great potential, but like all ideas, they can go wrong. They motivate, but in the wrong way. Frederick Herzberg, a management theorist, believes that motivation has to come from within the employee; he also believes that money in the case of a stock option will only motivate temporarily.[18]

EMPLOYEE CONCERN

In traditional corporate governance, employee involvement is limited to "one share, one vote" (directly or through proxies) exercised primarily at an annual meeting to choose a board and make decisions as defined in the by-laws.[19] But employee participation can involve much more than this. Referring back to the study of the forty-five companies with ESOPs, the evidence showed that regardless of company size, or the size of employee contributions, or even the percentage of the company owned by the ESOP, companies that instituted participation plans grew at a rate three or four times faster than companies that did not.[20] Furthermore, the number of meetings held in which labor and management could develop corporate plans and resolve their difficulties had an impact on performance.

Dalton Foundries in Warsaw, Indiana, was a family-owned company. When Matt Dalton, chairman of the company, started considering the future, he decided an ESOP would be the best choice. This choice would allow Dalton to withdraw gradually from the company as the employees took over. There are 540 employees at Dalton Industries; only 110 non-union employees are involved in the ESOP. CEO Ken Davidson and Matt Dalton are both committed to keeping employees involved. During monthly meetings employees are kept up to date on the financial happenings in the business. This information is private and not to be divulged to outsiders.[21]

Another aspect of involvement is participation groups. Dalton Foundries has twenty of these groups. Employees are given the opportunity to make improvements in the production process.

Another example is that of Weirton Steel. In 1984, Weirton's 7,000 employees bought 100 percent of the company. Weirton placed television monitors throughout the plant to keep everyone up to date on new developments and financial and production data. Weirton now employs 8,500 people and has shown a profit for 14 straight quarters, a record unmatched among integrated steelmakers.[22]

There are negative reasons for companies to choose employee ownership: to save a failing company, to prevent hostile takeovers, or even to induce employees to take wage concessions. One complaint is that companies implement ESOPs so pension plans can be terminated. Statistics show, however, that only 8 percent of companies choosing employee ownership terminated existing pension plans.[23]

Rosen has identified four factors that tie together what employee stock ownership plans do and need to bring about increased motivation, positive company spirit, growth in sales and production, and a bright future for the company.

1. The size of annual contributions to the ESOP (the typical company contributed an amount equivalent to just over 10 percent of pay)
2. The amount of employee participation in decisions affecting their jobs and company

3. The degree to which management believed that ownership was a good idea in its own right, aside from tax considerations

4. The frequency with which the company shared information with employees

Employee stock ownership plans are gaining momentum. There are presently 8,100 companies using ESOPs; only 5,000 were in existence in 1983.[24] The world is an ever-changing place and changing faster every day. This may be one of the biggest changes seen in the way business is done, and could possibly bring about the best working relationships ever seen in the United States.

NOTES

1. Corey Rosen, and Michael Quarry, "How Well Is Employee Ownership Working," *Harvard Business Review* (September–October 1987): 126.

2. Phillip Dewe, Stephen Dunn, and Ray Richardson, "Employee Share Option Schemes, Why Workers Are Attracted to Them," *Wall Street Journal*, 3 May, 1988, col. 2, 33.

3. Ibid.

4. Ralph E. Drtina and Marshall R. Gunsel, "Evaluating ESOPs: Spreading Risks and Ensuring Employee Acceptance," *SAM Advanced Management Journal* 53/1 (Winter 1988): 43–48.

5. Ibid., p. 44.

6. Ibid.

7. Anup Agrawal and Gershon N. Mandelker, "Managerial Incentives and Corporate Investments and Financing Decisions," *Journal of Finance* 42/4 (September 1987): 823–37.

8. Dewe, Dunn, and Richardson, "Employees Share Option Schemes."

9. Joan C. Szabo, "Small-Business Update," *Nation's Business* 76 (June 1988).

10. Corey Rosen, "A Close-Up View of ESOPs," *Foundary M & T* (September 1986): 32.

11. Ibid.

12. Douglas R. Brown, and Brian H. Kleiner, "Employee Ownership: Problems & Prospects," *Personnel Administrator* (December 1985): 786.

13. Rosen, "Close-Up View," p. 34.

14. Rosen and Quarry, "How Well Is Employee Ownership Working," p. 126.

15. Rosen, "Close-Up View," p. 34.

16. Rosen and Quarry, "How Well Is Employee Ownership Working," p. 127.

17. Graef S. Crystal and Fred K. Foulkes, "Don't Bail Out Underwater Options," *Fortune* 117 (March 14, 1988): 171–72.

18. Frederick Herzberg, *One More Time: How Do You Motivate Employees?"* 3d ed. (Plano, Tex.: Business Publications, 1986), pp. 282–97.

19. Brown and Kleiner, "Employee Ownership," p. 78.

20. Rosen and Quarry, "How Well Is Employee Ownership Working," p. 128.

21. Rosen, "Close-Up View," p. 35.

22. Ibid.

23. Brown and Kleiner, "Employee Ownership," p. 78.

24. Peter Larson, "Former Workers Primed to Buy Closed Alcoa Plant," *Dallas Times Herald* (December 25, 1983): A–39.

11

INSIDER TRADING

Insider trading is illicit profit making from the information obtained about any private corporate behavior before knowledge becomes public. The popularity of making easy money has made insider trading a powerful tool. The 1980s saw the Boesky scandal, "junk bonds," and "parking." The Securities and Exchange Commission (SEC) has played a major role in stopping the movement of insider trading, but the future portends more of this illegal practice. Even with this crackdown on insider traders, SEC can claim only a few victories. The limiting factor is that by law there is no clear definition of who an insider is and which practices are prohibited. The law insider traders are accused of breaking is the vague rule 10b-5 of section 10b of the Securities and Exchange Act of 1934. Rule 10b makes it "unlawful for any person to engage in any act that operates as a fraud or deceit upon any person, in connection with purchase or sale of any security."[1]

THE ORIGIN OF INSIDER TRADING

The question of where insider trading began is a puzzling one. Insider trading has only received media attention since the 1980s. In the early 1980s, SEC began to compile evidence that suggested insider trading. John M. Fedders, SEC's director of enforcement, brought fifty-one cases to court between 1980 and 1984. Fedders began to expose insider traders. Not only were they corporate executives, but bankers, lawyers, accountants, relatives, friends, and even government figures such as Deputy Secretary of Defense Paul Thayer. SEC, through extensive research, uncovered a typist at a law firm who made $50,000 in stock profits in one day by trading with the advanced knowledge that there would be a takeover.

Even with Fedders exposing the game of insider trading, the lure of easy money kept traders interested. The risk-reward ratio was particularly attractive, enhanced by the merger boom and the surge on option trading. Risk was virtually nil, and the convicted insider would only be forced to give back his profits and pay a $10,000 fine.[2] As insider trading became more popular, the market was threatened by the loss of millions of honest investors who believed in fair securities markets, where all participants play by the same rules.

We have defined insider trading as trading securities with knowledge of nonpublic information.[3] The act of insider trading, however, is not specifically prohibited by federal law. Instead, the definition is left up to the courts which decide what acts are considered insider trading.[4] This is why so many traders are not convicted.

A survey on awareness about insider trading conducted by Gary L. Tidwell and Abdul Aziz included 121 retail stockbrokers, 42 MBA students, and 153 undergraduate students. Seven scenarios were given, and those surveyed were to decide if insider trading had taken place. Surprisingly, the percentages among the three groups were fairly similar. In two questions, the undergraduates did better than the other two groups by at least 10 percent. This survey suggests that even people who operate in the business industry are not sufficiently educated. Because of this lack of education, many will fall prey to others who will use them as pawns in their illegal activity. They will end up taking the fall for smarter businesspeople. Those who take the blame for others can face a civil penalty up to three times the profits made, fines up to $100,000, and a jail term of up to five years.[5] All those involved in business need to be aware of what constitutes insider trading. Unfortunately, of those who do understand insider trading, many will try to get around the law. Congress needs to provide a clear, concise, statutory definition of insider trading.[6] However, changing the law alone will not stop people from committing the act. We also need to educate people in the securities game as well as the general public.

THE COURTS AND SEC

The courts have largely circumvented attempts made by SEC to control insider trading. They have sent a message to insider traders that even if prosecuted they can win. They have ruled against any agencies that have tried to prosecute outsiders who possess nonpublic information. The courts in the early 1980s made some critical rulings on who an insider is and under what circumstances a person violates rule 10b-5.

SEC charged thirteen officers, directors, and employees of Texas Gulf Sulphur with buying their company's stock three days before it publically announced a major copper strike. The Supreme Court let stand a lower court ruling that corporate officers and other insiders must not trade on private knowledge of major corporate developments until the news has been made open to the public. In 1980, SEC argued that a markup man for financial printer Vincent Chiarella was an insider when he traded in the securities of the targets of merger bids. The Supreme Court decided that Chiarella was not an insider because he had no relations with the companies that were merger targets. The determining factor of being an insider trader is establishing a loyalty to the shareholders of the company traded in by the person trading on the inside information. Chief Justice Warren Burger argued that Chiarella had misappropriated nonpublic information.[7]

In September 1983, Gilbert Lund, president of Verit Industries, became an insider of Pand F. Industries. When Verit was asked to participate in a new venture organized by Pand, Lund did not participate; however, he used knowledge to trade and make tremendous profits in Pand stock. The court ruled that Lund was guilty of insider trading because of his special relationship with Pand. In 1983, SEC charged that security analyst Raymond Dirks became an insider when he learned about an insurance fraud scheme at Equity Funding Corp. from a former corporate officer and thus violated 10b-5 by passing along confidential information to clients. However, the Supreme Court reversed a lower court ruling that convicted Dirks and again established that an insider must have a relationship to the stockholders. Also, the ruling proclaimed that a person who gets information from an insider becomes an insider only when the information is given improperly. The ruling was a certain victory for Dirks, but as a consequence insider trading was more difficult to enforce. The ruling clearly favored security analysts, who often pick up insider trading information from their research. It could also make it more difficult for SEC to prosecute outsiders who pick up information casually or when a company official asks their advice.[8]

After losing some well-represented cases involving insider traders, SEC recovered some lost ground when a second circuit court ruled that an outsider can be prosecuted for the misuse of information belonging to an employer.

THE BOESKY SCANDAL

The Boesky scandal will go down in history as the landmark case of insider trading in the 1980s. "The Wall Street Watergate" is an appropriate title for this scandal, which opened many flood gates for SEC. The scandal began on November 14, 1986. SEC had made public to the whole business world that Ivan Boesky, one of America's wealthiest stockmarket speculators, had been caught in an ongoing investigation for insider trading. To settle his own case, Boesky agreed to put $50 million in an escrow account for the benefit of investors harmed by his illegal trading. He also agreed to pay the U.S. Treasury a $50-million fine, an amount equal to nearly half of SEC's annual budget. Boesky also pleaded guilty to one court of unspecified criminal activity.[9] Finally, Boesky had to accept banishment for life from any professional stock trading, and still could face a possible five-year jail term.

Boesky arrived on Wall Street in 1966 at the L. F. Rothschild and Co. He was a true professional when it came to arbitrage trade. The "king of the arbitrageurs" would buy up target stock, hoping to back a successful takeover. By buying up the stock, he helped raiders by increasing the price of the stock. In such a case if all goes well the raiders will have found enough backing to make the takeover bid. This too will increase stock prices. The arbitrageur will then wait until the takeover bid becomes heated. When it reaches this point, the price of the stock peaks, and the arbitrageur dumps his stocks on the market at a tremendous profit.[10]

Arbitrage which is based on public knowledge of acquisition bids has long been recognized as a legitimate exercise in which professional traders assume much of the risk inherent in trading stocks involved in takeover battles. This is all perfectly legal until the rules are bent, which is why Boesky got caught. In 1975, Boesky started his own arbitrage firm, openly advertising to investors and hiring a public relations man. Boesky began to ride the arbitrage road to success at the beginning of the 1980s by investing large sums of money, earning the nickname of "piggy" on Wall Street. After Boesky had been caught for insider trading, the relentless wheeler dealer began to talk to authorities about all the stock trades he had made with the use of inside knowledge, and allowed regulators to eavesdrop on and tape his telephone conversations as he conducted business dealings. Because of this, Boesky began to shake up some of the biggest names in the corporate takeover business.[11]

After gathering information about dealings with Boesky, the U.S. Attorney's office in Manhattan had delivered at least a dozen subpoenas to important figures in the stock trading business. Among those who received documents were TWA chairman Carl Icahn. Icahn and Boesky had owned more than 50 percent of Gulf and Western's stock, and were rumored to have collaborated to run up the price of those shares by spreading rumors that the company was looked upon as a takeover target. Another well-known corporate raider, Victor Posner, was involved with Boesky in the New York City-based Fischbach Co. Boesky bought 13.4 percent of the company while Posner was paying $80 million to acquire control of the largest electrical contractor in the United States. The biggest name linked to the Boesky scandal was Michael Milken, a senior executive vice-president of New York City's Drexel, Burnham and Lambert investment firm. Milken is probably the most noted for the use of junk bonds, which have proven to be one of the most controversial financial instruments of the era. These low-grade, high-interest bonds have enabled corporate raiders to raise billions of dollars for ventures that have reshaped American business. Yet most investors have had persistent reservations about the safety of these securities. One concern is that there is too much underwriting and trading on junk bonds to finance takeover bids. Because borrowing money from the bank had too many strings attached, Milken could raise billions of dollars from investors who would buy junk bonds. Drexel's empire has greatly profited from Milken's junk bond strategy, but the controversy surrounding the firm about leaking inside information about takeovers could lead to its destruction—which brings the issue back to Boesky. Along with Milken, five other employees of Drexel, Burnham and Lambert as a corporation were issued subpoenas.

With the use of Boesky, U.S. attorney Rudolph W. Giuliani began his fight against Milken and Drexel. All of the charges were restricted almost entirely to Milken's relationship with Boesky and the information supplied by Boesky. The accusation against Drexel did not involve the junk bond market made so popular by the firm. Most of the evidence pointed toward an alleged "parking" scheme. In a parking strategy, an investor disguises ownership of securities, usually by arranging for another firm or individual to hold or trade them. The parker usually agrees to reimburse the collaborator for losses.[12] Milken would direct Boesky to take securities positions while Drexel would retain beneficial ownership. In 1984, deals with Fischbach and MCA were exposed first. In the Fischbach deal, Drexel had Boesky buy at 10 percent of Fischbach. This would free Posner, a Drexel client, from the pledge not to acquire Fischbach. Later on, Posner would buy the company. Drexel then got Boesky to buy MCA stock, which helped another Drexel client, Golden Nugget, dispose of a large position in MCA. In 1985, Boesky parked a large block of Phillips Petroleum stock with the size of his securities positions. Again in 1985, Drexel got Boesky to buy at least 5 percent of Harris Graphics in order to attract bidders to the company. A buyout of this company would profit many Drexel employees who had invested. Government supporters argued that convicting Drexel and Milken, even on just a few violations, would be a victory. After all, tax evasion was enough to send Al Capone to prison.[13]

In September 1988, SEC, after two years of investigation, charged Drexel and Milken with a scheme to manipulate the market in at least sixteen big-ticket securities deals. The investigation alleged that Drexel worked almost exclusively with Boesky to bid up stock prices of many takeover targets, profiting from inside information about many different offers. Three other Drexel employees including Victor Posner were charged with securities laws violations. The most damaging charges came after SEC got tired of waiting for Giuliani to act and charged Drexel with working in a conspiracy with Boesky to bid up stock prices of many takeover targets. Drexel agreed on December 21, 1988, to plead guilty to six counts of criminal fraud, and pay $650 million in fines.[14]

SEC used Boesky to uncover more names of those involved in insider trading. Next was a former managing director of Drexel, Dennis Levine. Boesky's relationship was uncovered when Levine was charged in May 1986 with illegal trading. SEC charged Levine with illegal trading profits which added up to $12.6 million during the beginning of his relationship in 1985. Levine began to feed Boesky tips on upcoming mergers, acquisitions, and corporate restructurings that were likely to lead to increased stock prices for some of the companies involved. Levine was to get 50 percent if his tip led to Boesky's making an initial investment in a stock, and 10 percent if his information concerned a stock that Boesky had already invested in.[15] All of the profits were made between February 1985 and February 1986.

Levine was a young investment banker in New York, and used many of his peers to work with Boesky on profit schemes. Using Levine's tips, Boesky made $4 million by buying Nabisco Brands before it was taken over by R. J. Reynolds. He earned another $4.1 million when he bought the Houston Natural Gas Corp. Finally, Boesky made another $975,000 on advance word that FMC Corp. was going to restructure its financial base. Levine's covert role began to surface as early as May 1985, when an anonymous letter from Caracas to the Merrill Lynch investment house alleged trading irregularities on the part of two company employees in Venezuela. Both had since left the firm.[16] SEC went to work, finding the mastermind of the case was Levine. This opened many gates for SEC. The Boesky scandal has definitely caused problems for many people on Wall Street. Boesky was a greedy person, with no consideration for anybody who got in the way of making some cash. Boesky beat his competitors by the willingness to pay a higher price. The boldness displayed by Boesky was a farce, for he knew far more than anyone else, and therefore never really took any risks.

ILLEGAL PARKING

In this strategy, an investor disguises his ownership of securities by arranging for another individual or firm to hold or trade on his behalf.[17] Parking is used to concoct phony tax losses for the disguised investor. Under this disguise, the investor allegedly sells his securities at a loss to his stockbroker, but in reality the broker is only serving the wishes of the investor. Other parking strategies involve evading capital law limits, which is the practice of an investor dividing the profits gained on a transaction with his broker—and the division only exists on paper. In return, the broker receives a substantial commission for compliance. The practice of parking has increased over the last few years due to limited sanctions.[18]

WHY INSIDER TRADING WORKS

Why does insider trading occur? The answer is quite obvious—it offers a quick, large return on investment. When people begin insider trading, others can see something "going on" because it increases the stock prices closer toward "real worth."[19] When those who have the nonpublic information begin to trade, others will investigate the increased volume of purchases. Combining these findings with other information, they will make inferences regarding the exchanges. As the number of people trading increases, the price will increase to the actual worth of the stock.[20]

INSIDER ETHICS

Though insider traders work hard to gain profit, what they are doing is unethical because these people basically write their own checks for the work they have done.[21] Genuine insiders should be compensated for the work they do to meet the overall goals of the organization—not for information they happen to stumble across in the course of business activities.

Another ethical consideration in insider trading involves outsiders, those who gain information in the course of their job but are not employed by the company (such as the editor of a magazine).[22] By misappropriation, such individuals, occupying a position of trust and confidence, may take confidential nonpublic information from an organization.[23]

How far will people go to obtain insider information? Will they risk their jobs for it? S. G. Rudy Ruderman had been *Business Week* broadcast editor since 1981. As broadcast editor, he received information early every day from a brokerage firm he had traded with on a regular basis. Ruderman had apparently made trades prior to the magazine's official 2 P.M. release. This was a violation of *Business Week*'s requirement that all securities be disclosed to the editor-in-chief, and a ban on trading stocks of companies mentioned in the magazine until one week after the cover date. Ruderman was subsequently fired on April 12.[24]

Another case of insider trading was all in the family. In this case, Carl Karcher, founder of Carl Karcher Enterprises, Inc., tipped off family members that third-quarter earnings of Carl's Jr. (fast food outlets) were going to go down sharply due to the expansion into the Texas market. Karcher advised sixteen of his relatives to sell their shares of stock. The National Securities Association of Securities Dealers market surveillance computer noticed a higher volume of trading on the Karcher Enterprise stock than usual, and the association sought to investigate the increase. Later SEC filed charges of insider trading against Karcher and his family members. However, Karcher's attorney contended that the increase in the volume of trading was coincidental.[25] Even though Karcher confided only in his relatives, what he did was wrong. Other people who purchased Karcher stock suffered the losses, while the Karcher clan is still one of the wealthiest families in California. These two cases are only a few of the myriad of cases which involve insider trading. Many are more severe and cost individuals and society much more money.

THE EFFECTS OF UNETHICAL BUSINESS BEHAVIOR

Cases involving insider trading not only deceive companies and shareholders, but society as well. While only a few get rich, the majority suffers. When an individual engages in insider trading, he thinks only of how much money he can make in a short period of time. Such insiders steal from the people who initially owned the stock. However, the long-range effects of insider trading can be detrimental. People may lose faith in the market, and no longer invest in securities. If the number of people is large enough, the volume of stocks being traded will be lower which will in turn alarm others in the market. If panic occurs, people will pull out of the market. Once the bottom drops out of the market and panic spreads, a depression could occur. In that case the banks and the government cannot back up their notes, and may go bankrupt. This, of course, is an extreme case, but there is a possibility it could occur. If it did, there are very few who would escape aside from the elite rich. The point is that a "quick buck" may have long-range disadvantages for the individual and society.

Another perspective from which to approach this topic is through the concept of self-interest. Self-interest is one of the underlying principles of capitalism. However, there is a difference between self-interest and selfishness. If a person earns money and power within legal limits, he deserves to live the life of luxury. But insider trading is not within legal boundaries. Individuals obtaining profit from such activity are not entrepreneurs, but criminals. These individuals should be treated like other criminals. The information they are stealing is not petty or of little value. Many people are affected by this premeditated crime. Individuals engaging in this activity know exactly what they are doing, thinking only about profitable outcomes with little regard for the consequences. Stricter laws need to be enacted by the government. Not only should violators pay large fines, but should serve mandatory prison sentences of at least five years. Perhaps if these individuals knew of such strict laws, they would be more hesitant to get involved in illegal activity. The laws regarding insider trading must be strict enough that lawyers will be unable to get their clients off with paying only fines. However, society needs to pressure Congress to increase the severity of the sentences. Only if a significant portion of the population speaks will any changes ensue.

INSIDER TRADING IN THE WORKPLACE

It is tragic that individuals entrusted with nonpublic information often use it for their own personal advantage. People of such status are put in these positions because they are qualified and can be trusted with confidential information. Some type of oath should be taken by every person with access to nonpublic information. Violation of such an oath should ban an individual from working in any area involving nonpublic information. A severe penalty should be imposed as well. If we cannot trust people in responsible positions, we may feel that we cannot trust any individuals involved in business activities. This would lead to an unraveling of business. If this occurs, business deals among companies may cease to exist; everyone wary of the other. Another possible effect might be that companies may not divulge information until the day an action occurs, which would mean the public would not find out until a few days later due to the time it would take to broadcast.

CORRUPTION IN BUSINESS

Insider trading is only part of the corruption in business. Corruption exists in almost every area of business, whether a small-time businessman is receiving kickbacks or a top executive benefits from a hostile takeover. Is there no limit to what these people will do to make a few dollars? Unfortunately, there is not. These people believe it is "the American way." Capitalism is a system in which wealth is measured by who controls the most. So then, is our society corrupt because of its economic system? Those who initially developed the idea of capitalism did not have corrupt practices in mind. In ancient Greece, the people believed in a pure democracy, but saw business as evil. Perhaps these people saw something we do not. Nonetheless, business itself is not evil. Individuals *within* the business make it evil. Each of us has a certain amount of greed. For example, if we win $100 and we have the opportunity to triple that amount or keep the $100, most of us would take the chance to triple it. However, we are gambling with our own money. Big business gambles not only with its own money, but also with the money of others. Many average Americans take a stab at the stock market or other investments in order to get ahead. When corporations or powerful individuals try to make more money for themselves, they manipulate the small investor. As the powerful manipulate, they gain more power and acquire more wealth. On the other hand, the average American loses out once again.

Just how far will the rich go to attain money and power? Shows like "Dallas," "Dynasty," "Knots Landing," and "Falcon Crest" may not be totally accurate in their portrayal of what goes on in the business world, but some of the dealings may stem from real life. How many of these "make believe" events actually occur in the course of everyday business? Do we really know? Some of the episodes of these shows do stem from current events. For example, in a few episodes of "Knots Landing" an insider trading scam occurred in which two of the main characters were "scratching" each other's back so they could have it all. Both characters were caught by a state investigator. However, expensive lawyers got both characters off through the use of a scapegoat. So maybe these shows are more accurate than we think. The rich on news and television specials are shown in their limosines and extravagant homes spending large amounts of money. How did they get where they are? Was it hard work, or was it deceit and manipulation? Whether it was hard work or deceit, it is plain to see that the gap between the rich and the poor is widening, while the middle class is becoming extinct. Perhaps one day the poor will get fed up and retaliate in one form or another to bring down the aristocracy.

THE EFFECT OF CORRUPTION ON SOCIETY

Oftentimes corrupt business deals have an adverse effect on the natural environment. Every day we hear news stories about the hole in the ozone layer, air pollution, destruction of the rain forest, and toxic waste dumps. Most of these problems have been and are caused by corporations. Do those people who make decisions regarding the destruction of the environment neglect to see the long-term effects of what they are doing? Most executives tend to disregard the environment in order to decrease costs, and attempt methods that are illegal and covert to meet the goals of the corporation. Because these decision makers want to gain immediate gratification the environment suffers. What is so ironic about these decision makers is that they are giving to causes to save the environment. Perhaps they are trying to atone for their guilt. What these people and the rest of us refuse to see are the effects our actions have on the environment; some may be irreversible. We are all to blame for the state of our environment because we purchase products that destroy our environment, especially the ozone layer. We all must take actions to save our world from becoming extinct.

CORPORATE GOVERNANCE EDUCATION

Throughout this chapter, businesses have been blamed for defrauding U.S. citizens. However, we are all to blame because we have not pushed our legal system to enforce the laws regulating corporate activities. How can we blame individuals if we do not know what we are blaming them for? People need to educate themselves by watching the national news and reading business magazines and newspapers. The more informed society is, the better position we are in to challenge corporations and executives. Once we are educated, we can force the legislature to enact laws and provide stricter guidelines for corporations. Until we decide to go through this process, corporations will continue to rob society.

CONCLUSION

Although SEC seems to have taken a major step forward in the fight against insider traders with the Boesky scandal, SEC wants Congress to rewrite the current law. SEC feels that the sanctions in the current law are weak and ineffective. The law currently maintains that the violator pay back any profit. Most cases are closed as soon as the defendant either admits or denies guilt and gives up the profit. The House has taken some action and passed a bill raising the penalties to triple damages. The Senate is considering a bill by New York Republican Senator Alfonse D'Amato that defines insider trading to eliminate the requirement to prove personal benefits.[26] SEC's strategy in its war on insider trading is improving. Even though the Supreme Court has not ruled on the charge of misappropriating information, the agency can hold against offenders the power to win lower court cases. Although many of the criminals go free, SEC will continue to press the issue against insider trading.

The 1980s brought a new breed of trader to Wall Street. Greed seems to have replaced old-fashioned hard work. Insider trading and takeover bids have become common practice. The Boesky scandal will probably be remembered not only because of the laws broken, but for opening up an unknown world to SEC. In order for SEC to deal with this problem, penalties are going to have to become more severe. It is a matter of ethics. Is insider trading the choice? Is cheating and greed the standard?

NOTES

1. Arlen Hershman, "Insider Trading—Why It Can't Be Stopped," *Duns Business Monthly* (June 1984): 52.

2. Ann Reilly, "Inside Crackdown," *Fortune* (May 14, 1984): 144.

3. Gary L. Tidwell, and Abdul Aziz, "Insider Trading: How Well Do You Understand the Current Status of the Law?" *California Management Review* (Summer 1988): 117.

4. Ibid., p. 115.

5. Ibid.

6. Ibid., p. 126.

7. Hershman, "Insider Trading," p. 56.

8. "A Victory for Raymond Dirks," *Duns Business Monthly* (August 1986): 22.

9. Larry Martz, "True Greed," *Newsweek* (December 1, 1986): 49.

10. Abbass Alkhafaji, *A Stakeholder Approach to Corporate Governance: Managing in a Dynamic Environment"* (New York: Quorum, 1989), p. 170.

11. George Russel, "Going after the Crooks," *Time* (December 1986): 49.

12. Chris Welles, "Just How Corrupt Is Wall Street," *Business Week* (January 9, 1989): 35.

13. Chris Welles, "Just How Damaging Is the Case Against Drexel Burnham," *Business Week* (November 28, 1988): 61.

14. Ibid., p. 34.

15. Martz, "True Greed," p. 52.

16. Russel, "Going after the Crooks," p. 54.

17. Welles, "Just How Corrupt Is Wall Street," p. 35.

18. Ibid.

19. Leo Herzel, and Leo Katz, "Insider Trading: Who Loses?" *Lloyds Book Review* (July 1987): 15.

20. Ibid., p. 16.

21. Ibid.

22. Ibid., p. 18.

23. Tidwell and Aziz, "Insider Trading," p. 17.

24. Chris Welles, and Lawrence J. Tell, "Inside Wall Street: The Probe Hits Home," *Business Week* (August 29, 1989): 30–31.

25. Ellen Paris, "Family Ties," *Forbes* (July 11, 1988): 62.
26. Russel, "Going after the Crooks," p. 54.

BIBLIOGRAPHY

Alkhafaji, Abbass. *A Stakeholder Approach to Corporate Governance: Managing in a Dynamic Environment.* New York: Quorum, 1989.

Gleckman, Howard. "The SEC Makes Its Move on Drexel and Milken," *Business Week* (September 19, 1988): 32.

Hershman, Arlen. "Insider Trading—Why It Can't be Stopped," *Duns Business Monthly* (June 1984): 48–57.

Martz, Larry. "True Greed," *Newsweek* (December 1, 1986): 48–52.

"A Victory for Ray Dirks," *Duns Business Monthly* (August 1983): 22–23.

Pauly, David. "Just How Damning Is the Case against Drexel Burnham." *Business Week* (November 24, 1986): 68.

Reilly, Ann. "Inside Crackdown." *Fortune* (May 14, 1984): 143–44.

Russel, George. "Going after the Crooks." *Time* (December 1, 1986): 49–56.

Scheibla, Shirley. "Split in the SEC." *Barron's* (May 2, 1983): 48–49.

Stern, Richard. "The Inside Inside Story." *Forbes* (March 12, 1984): 62–63.

Welles, Chris. "Just How Corrupt Is Wall Street." *Business Week* (January 9, 1989): 34–36.

Worthy, Ford. "Money and Markets," *Fortune* (December 22, 1986): 27–29.

12

International Acquisitions

Due to the attractiveness of international acquisitions, the United States had invested heavily in foreign markets in the past. Foreign investment reached a peak in 1930, but rapidly declined during the Depression. Between 1946 and 1957, foreign investment began to grow again with government loans and private investments. The years 1957 to 1970 were a period of direct investment, which marked the beginning of multinational enterprise. During this period, U.S. investment was at its highest ever, the majority being the result of direct investment.[1] Direct investment in the United States continued to grow during the 1980s. The large current account deficit experienced by the United States resulted in an excessive accumulation of dollars in the hands of foreigners; many of these dollars flowed back into the United States in the form of direct investment.[2] Direct foreign investment, which is the main focus of this chapter, can be defined as a long-term equity investment (purchase of assets such as land, plant, or securities) in a foreign firm that gives the investor managerial control over that firm.

REASONS FOR ACQUISITIONS

In 1987 a record $42 billion was spent by foreign investors to acquire U.S. plants, equipment, services, and real estate. This figure rose 68 percent from the previous year. Foreign investments in the United States seemed to be spurred by the cheap dollar, political stability, and sharply lower stock prices.[3]

An international acquisition takes place when an established group purchases enough stock in a company located in another country to gain control over that company. The established firm is likely to acquire a company that is related to its own product line. In general, there are three main reasons for acquisitions. The first is that the acquiring firm feels that it is essential to survival. The management of acquiring firms is quick to make restructuring decisions in order to improve the efficiency and productivity of the company. Diversification is a second reason for acquisitions. Diversification allows subsidiary companies to be easily liquidated for profits. The third reason is that acquisitions result in favorable profit. The acquiring firm can resell the holdings in the company at a higher price.

There are a number of motives for a company to obtain an acquisition as opposed to building their own facilities. One motive would be that the firm will have no startup problems. Facilities and resources are already available. Since the firm already exists, another motive for an acquisition is the desire for greater growth in a shorter period of time. Acquisitions do not add capacity in the market; acquisitions reduce costs and risks; and acquisitions may save money and time that would otherwise be needed to develop goodwill and a name in a foreign country.[4]

Some companies are still buying unrelated businesses they do not know and cannot run. Reasons for this vary. One reason is to get to overfunded pension plans. This was illustrated when the Tengelmann Group of West Germany purchased the controlling interest in the Great A&P Tea Company. The supermarket chain was in financial trouble with stores closing across the country. A&P had built a large overfunded pension plan for its retired employees. This plan had been set up for employees only. But upon acquisition the Tengelmann Group obtained control of the pension fund. The Tengelmann Group then purchased an insurance annuity program which agreed to pay retired employees a fixed amount each month. They then used the pension fund money to refurbish the A&P supermarket chain. The Tengelmann Group successfully turned A&P around and is now making acquisitions of its own. The Tengelmann story can be viewed as a success but there have been other companies which have not handled the same situation as well. Some companies have gained control of pension funds and have not used the money to benefit the organization.

RISK

There is a great risk involved in trying to diversify by acquisition. Reasons why a company would want to diversify are to smooth out earning cycles, invest excess cash, or attempt to boost growth in earnings per share. This sounds like a good idea but there is a very high failure rate when this program is implemented. A study was conducted by three employees of McKinsey & Company Inc. The study focused on sixty industrial companies in Great Britain. Each company was attempting to incorporate diversification programs through acquisition. The study showed that there was a mortality rate of about 75 percent. This rate is for acquisitions of large, unrelated organizations. This rate decreases as the size of the acquisition decreases. This also has a direct effect on the stakeholders of a company. Acquisition activity destroys shareholder wealth in both companies. Acquiring companies lose one to 7 percent of their stock value in the year after a merger or acquisition.[5] To increase its own shareholder value, the acquiring company must be able to significantly increase the operating performance of the company it has acquired. Due to the lack of expertise and large amounts of capital, this task is rarely accomplished. The style of management practiced by the acquiring company must also be taken into consideration.

The parent company cannot take a laissez-faire attitude when it comes to managing the acquired company. The idea that the company will run itself is nothing more than wishful thinking. If that approach is taken the company will soon be in financial turmoil. Another approach is to simply replace the management team. This approach can lead to even worse problems. Therefore, the question still remains: How can an effective management team be built? A compromise is necessary if the company is to run effectively. Motivation in management may decline. Management may no longer have the same incentive to perform under the new arrangement as it did when the company was more independent.

RESISTING TAKEOVERS

The most popular tactic for resisting an attempted takeover is to convince local and state officials to come to the company's defense. Local governments will usually do everything they can for a hometown company even though they realize that it is a losing battle. Most politicians know that when they come to the aid of management all they are doing is prolonging the takeover and helping the CEO get a higher selling price. This does not mean that local officials should stand back and watch the takeover. The restructuring of corporate America, brought on by the takeover wars, hits local facilities the hardest. Factories and office buildings are closed, and workers are informed of layoffs as corporations are forced to economize. John Peterson, a senior director of the Government Finance Officers Association research center, believes that "local governments are increasingly concerned about their economic base and employment.'"[6] Most of the laws passed by states fail to deter take-overs.

The best that local officials can do for their constituents is to make a deal with the acquiring company. Such deals could include employment guarantees and assurance that the company will stay in the area. These deals can be struck so long as officials agree to drop legal proceedings and to ease resistance to the takeover. Also, public officials can use their leverage to influence corporate decisions. This leverage can take the form of tax concessions and infrastructure improvements. These opportunities must be seized if local governments hope to protect their economic base.

FOREIGN INVESTMENT IN U.S. FIRMS

The history of foreign investment in the United States is a diversified one. From the 1930s to the 1970s, portfolio investment was the most common foreign investment in the United States. Portfolio investment can be defined as a long-term investment (more than one year) when the ownership percentage is less than 10 percent, which does not give the investor control. From 1965 through the 1970s, portfolio investments were still more common than direct investments by foreign companies, but direct investments dramatically increased in the 1970s and 1980s.[7]

Advantages of Investment in U.S. Firms

The first advantage for foreign countries is the weak dollar in the United States. This weak dollar had reduced the cost of manufacturing in the United States compared to a strong-currency country. Another advantage foreign firms have is the result of the Tax Reform Act of 1986. Many acquisitions occurred because the act made it advantageous to complete acquisitions of existing U.S. enterprises by the end of the year. Also stock prices can be an advantage to foreign investors.[8]

When a foreign investor decides to acquire a U.S. company, it is likely that the stock prices will go up, thus increasing profits. In addition to raising their own stock prices in the acquired firm, foreign countries have the advantage of the low stock prices of U.S. firms resulting from the stock market crash of 1987. The crash has caused U.S. firms to sell their assets at great discount prices.[9] European countries have an advantage over other countries in investing in U.S. firms due to the recent economic recovery in Europe. This recovery left many European companies with large amounts of cash which they are unable to invest in Europe. The hungriest country seems to be Great Britain. A strong British pound helped to fuel this activity. The pound had an increase of 27 percent against the dollar in 1988. Another advantage that British companies has is that they do not have to write off earnings of goodwill that new acquisitions produce on their financial statements. U.S. companies, in contrast, must write off goodwill against profits penalizing reported earnings for the year. Raising capital for these acquisitions was helped by Great Britain's bull market. Corporations raised the money they needed by simply issuing extra shares. For now, the crash has killed this technique for the British, just as it gave pause to takeovers in the United States.[10] All acquisitions in recent years have forced companies that have escaped a takeover thus far to restructure their organizations. Cutting costs, controlling inventories, and proper financing are all parts of the restructuring process. This has management looking for new ways of improving efficiency. Deborah Allen Oliver, president of Claremont Economics Institute, states that "the merger-acquisition wave definitely improves efficiency; you get rid of whole layers of management, you get rid of one corporate headquarters, and you strip the company of the junk."[11]

Most of the restructuring in the United States has taken place in heavy industry—machinery equipment manufacturing, chemicals, and natural resources.[12] But no area is immune from foreign buyers. In 1985 foreign-owned companies accounted for 8.5 percent of all U.S. manufacturing sales, up from the 1980 figure of 5.1 percent. Foreign control over manufacturing sales is on the rise and will probably continue through the 1990s.

Foreign companies seem to have an interest in the chemical industry, where they control more than 33 percent of the U.S. sales market. Acquisitions in the communications industry are seen as protection in case the economy falls into a recession.

Many companies have gotten away from trying to diversify into areas in which they have no experience. Many companies are now trying to sell back acquisition mistakes to companies already in that area. Many companies are looking for acquisitions that can best utilize their present management skills and resources. Getting away from portfolio management and moving toward specialization can help a company become more efficient, benefiting both the company and the economy.

Disadvantages

The Department of Commerce stated that for the first quarter of 1988, foreign investors earned more in this country than U.S. investors earned overseas. As a result of increasing foreign investment, the United States is paying more in interest and dividends to foreigners. These payments are so much more that they now exceed the interest and dividends paid to U.S. companies.[13] A second disadvantage for the United States when foreign companies acquire U.S. firms is that the trend of acquisitions over the long run will limit the growth of exports from the United States. If the growth of exports is limited, it will make the trade deficit more difficult to eliminate.[14] Foreign investors also have disadvantages. Management style may need to change to satisfy different customers and to adapt to unfamiliar technology. Also, companies have a tendency to acquire unprofitable firms in the belief that they can turn them around with new management. Unfortunately, despite high hopes, these acquired firms generally fail.[15]

U.S. INVESTMENT IN FOREIGN COUNTRIES

Even though foreign investment in the United States is increasing, U.S. investment in foreign countries is also common. Among the advantages are the decreasing time and cost for market entry. U.S. firms can penetrate the market more quickly and deeply in other countries. Another advantage is that wages are lower than they are in the United States.[16] In addition to home-grown talent being cheaper, laborers are sufficiently skilled and more knowledgeable about their markets than U.S. executives. It has been a recent trend to expand aggressively overseas and to rely more on local managers.[17] Also, the concepts of meeting foreign competitors on their own turf with a home-grown product is becoming accepted worldwide.

Some of the disadvantages of U.S. firms acquiring foreign firms are similar to the disadvantages previously mentioned. For example, there are problems with management style. Companies must be able to adapt their products and marketing techniques to customers in different cultures. U.S. firms receive low payoffs in comparison with other opportunities of market penetration.[18] Another disadvantage are trade barriers; U.S. firms must comply with foreign government and legal policies. For example, many foreign countries have barriers which limit acceptance of certain industries in a country.[19] Finally, foreign firms may be less similar to the U.S. company than it appears on the surface. The U.S. company may then run into unexpected and costly problems and fail.

An example of a U.S. firm acquiring a foreign firm is the acquisition of Banyu Pharmaceutical Co. of Tokyo by Merck & Co., the fifth largest drug maker in the United States. This acquisition was the largest ever in Japan, which is a great achievement considering the country's strict purchase policies.[20] An example of a foreign firm acquiring a U.S. firm is the acquisition of Joseph E. Seagram & Sons and Tropicana Products by the Canada-owned firm Seagram Co. Ltd. This investment is ranked as the largest foreign investment in the United States.[21]

THE FUTURE

The future seems to portend increased direct investment in foreign firms. The big firms are still actively involved in exporting, but the wave of future is production abroad. Corporations will begin to globalize their production more than ever, spreading employment, earnings, and technology to other countries.[22] Globalization has shortened the gap between product introduction and foreign production. Many companies design their products for simultaneous production and sale here and abroad.[23]

In the years to come, companies will be facing larger, better-financed, and more strategically oriented competitors. Generally, a global strategy is built on a foundation of solid business information. Suggestions for a coherent global strategy include monitoring technical journals; attending symposiums; tracking patents; and establishing an effective global communications network to convey information to members of the company in all departments, including the departments which operate overseas.[24] Other essential factors in global market success are a reputation for the best quality and service in the industry, having the most innovative people in the organization, and establishing international links for an exchange of technology.[25]

Another future trend in relation to international acquisitions is increased research and development. R&D will increase in three select areas[26]: (1) industries which are currently favored by changing world prices (e.g., producers of energy-saving products); (2) industries which are able to capitalize on continuing breakthroughs in basic research (e.g., bioengineering); and (3) industries producing income-elastic goods for which demand can be expected to expand as incomes in developing countries increase.

As firms become more committed to their international acquisitions, the need for information becomes more important. There are several reasons why a firm should invest in marketing research and product development. First of all, good research can prevent costly mistakes.[27] Research can ensure that the company's name will be well received. It is important for a firm to establish and maintain a good global image to be successful. Marketing research can identify opportunities as well as risks. For example, how much demand there is for a product may determine if marketing the product internationally is profitable. Finally, decisions about business structure can be improved with marketing research. For example, through research a company may be better able to decide if an acquisition or a joint venture may be more favorable.

Product development is just as important in international markets. International markets must design products to satisfy the needs of their consumers. This will take much planning and development since it involves knowing the needs and wants of consumers in entirely different cultures. The major problem with product development is the problem of self-reference criterion (SRC), that is, when a manager uses the home country frame of reference while making decisions about foreign markets. Since cultures differ dramatically, products can fail if managers are not aware of the self-reference criterion.

International acquisitions in the future will also being about changes in interaction with host governments. A firm wishing to acquire a foreign company must initially investigate the type and stability of the country's government. The acquiring firm must then learn about established legal requirements in the foreign firm. Legal restrictions can be imposed on product components, labeling, packaging, pricing, advertising, promotion, and distribution. After all, if this information is considered, the product can be successfully developed. Foreign investors will increasingly become involved in more government regulations and those countries which find it difficult to cooperate with host governments may suffer great losses.[28]

CONCLUSION

In conclusion, it is clear that there are two sides to the acquisitions issue. The acquisitions war has benefited corporate America in the form of restructuring. This "benefit" is actually the job of management and the board of directors. These individuals must run the organization effectively and efficiently. Apparently this responsibility has been forgotten by many managements in corporate America. It took a slap in the face by some raiders here in America and in foreign countries to wake them up. Carl Icahn, a famous raider-manager, believes American CEOs are an example of reverse Darwinism—the survival of the unfittest. If this is true it is time for a restructuring of corporate governance.

Next American companies must be legally protected from foreign acquisition. These laws should be set up not to protect the name of the company or the CEO but the workers. Employment protection and plant closing laws should be implemented to protect communities and the people who live there.

NOTES

1. Franklin R. Root, *International Trade and Investment* (Cincinnati: South-Western, 1973), p. 259.

2. Michael R. Czinkota, Pietra Rivoli, and Ikka A. Ronkainen, *International Business* (Chicago: Dryden, 1989), p. 63.

3. "The 100 Largest Foreign Investments in the U.S.," *Forbes* (July 25, 1988): 240.

4. Abbass F. Alkhafaji, *A Stakeholder Approach to Corporate Governance: Managing in a Dynamic Environment* (New York: Quorum, 1989), pp. 255–56.

5. "For Better or for Worse," *Business Week* (January 12, 1987): 38–40.

6. Alkhafaji, *Stakeholder Approach*, p. 256.

7. "Takeover Wars: What the Hometown Can Do—And Can't," *Business Week* (September 19, 1988).

8. Root, *International Trade and Investment*, p. 531.

9. "Overseas Spending by U.S. Companies Sets Record Pace," *New York Times* (May 20, 1988): I1:1; "U.S. Direct Investment Abroad, Reverse Investment, Both Up 13%," *Business America* (July 6, 1988): 9.

10. "Investors Face Risk on Expectations Holders Abroad with Big Stakes Will Buy U.S. Firms," *Wall Street Journal* (May 1, 1988), 71; 3.

11. Alkhafaji, p. 258.

12. "The Top 200 Deals" *Business Week*, April 15, 1988, p. 49.

13. "For Better or for Worse," *Business Week*, Jan. 12, 1987, p. 38–40.

14. "U.S. Statisticians Change Investors' Earnings Results," *Wall Street Journal*, June 16, 1988, 12;4.

15. *New York Times*, May 20, 1988: I1:1.

16. Alkhafaji, p. 258.

17. *New York Times*, May 20, 1988, I1: 1.

18. "A Special News Report on People and Their Jobs in Offices, Fields, and Factories," *Wall Street Journal*, May 3, 1988, 1; 5.

19. *New York Times*, May 20, 1988, I1: 1.

20. Alkhafaji, p. 259.

21. *New York Times*, May 20, 1988, I1: 1.

22. Alkhafaji, p. 257.

23. "The 100 Largest Foreign Investments in the U.S.", Forbes, July 25, 1988, p. 240.

24. *New York Times*, May 20, 1988, I1: 1.

25. "Strategies For Playing the Global Game," *New York Times*, June 26, 1988, III 3: 1.

26. Ibid., III 3: 1.

27. Peter J. Buckley, The Future of the Multinational Enterprise (New York: Holmes & Meier Publishers, Inc., 1976), p. 103.

28. Philip R. Cateora, Marketing: An International Perspective (Illinois: Richard D. Irwin, Inc., 1987), p. 39.

13

PRIVATIZATION

Since 1980, privatization has been increasing worldwide. Its effects and limitations have been discussed and debated by those in both the public and the private sectors. However, in spite of these debates, privatization has increased. During the Reagan administration, the prevailing belief was that the private sector could deliver better quality goods and services at lower prices with greater efficiency. With that belief, America was headed on the road to privatization.

DEFINITION

Privatization is the transfer of federal properties and activities to the private sector, while at the same time reducing the government's role as a creator of markets.[1] It may involve introducing or increasing competition, reducing obstacles to it, or selling state-controlled enterprises in the open market at a value negotiated by the buyer and the seller.[2]

Robert Poole believes that we can privatize only the financing of a service, as when shifting from tax funding to user fees. Or we can privatize only the delivery of the service, leaving the funding to the government, by means of contracting out. Or we can privatize both the funding and the delivery, which is sometimes called service shedding.

In this case the government gets out altogether, leaving the service to be provided in the marketplace on a competitive basis.[3]

There has been renewed interest in privatization recently because many feel that Uncle Sam has gotten too big, too expensive, and too much like "Big Brother." In addition, the interest stems from a belief that an amicable arrangement between the private and public sectors might boost productivity and efficiency, while at the same time offering more opportunities and satisfaction for the public.

THE IMPORTANCE OF PRIVATIZATION

The study of privatization is important for several reasons. First, privatization has several significant economic effects. Second, private sectors are more cost-efficient and more profitable (at least for some people). Finally, privatization affects society.

In the public sector, employees do not have a direct interest in the outcomes of their actions. However, in the private sector, employees feel the consequences of their actions directly. In a private enterprise, owners are going to be more concerned with the gains and losses of the company, since they will be directly affected by them. The assets of private enterprises are owned by individuals who are free to use and transfer these assets as long as this activity is legal. In a public enterprise, owners of the assets are the taxpayers.

When private enterprises produce goods and services which consumers demand at costs lower than market prices, the private enterprise is going to profit. However, if costs exceed market prices, then losses are incurred. Private enterprise owners are directly affected by the actions of their firms. Therefore, private enterprise owners are going to ensure profits from their firms.[4]

Private enterprise firms are more cost-effective than public firms. It costs twice as much to produce goods and services in a public enterprise. In a public enterprise, sales per employee are lower; adjusted profits per employee are lower; physical production per employee is lower; taxed paid per employee are lower; profits per dollar of total assets are lower; sales per employee grow at a slower rate; and more companies generate accounting losses than in a private enterprise.[5] Private enterprises are more efficient in terms of economics, costs, and profits.

In a public enterprise, loss-making activities can be supported. For example, public enterprises receive subsidies to employ people when it is not actually profitable for the company to employ additional people. In a private enterprise, those subsidies are not available. Public enterprises generally engage in profitable activities and leave meeting social needs to other enterprises. Also, public enterprises are more able to provide services to underdeveloped areas than private enterprises because gains and losses are more dispersed among the owners.

The United States is not unique in pursuing privatization. Many other countries have gone this route, including Japan and the Americas. Even socialist countries like the Soviet Union and China are moving along the privatization path. Great Britain, under Margaret Thatcher, has made the most impressive strides in this direction—in fact, it is one of the main themes of her administration.

METHODS OF PRIVATIZATION

There are three basic methods used for privatization. In the first one, the government sells assets outright. Good examples of this occurred recently when Jaguar was sold in Great Britain and Conrail was sold in the United States.

Another technique, contracting out, involves private firms entering into contracts with the government to provide goods and/or services for use by the public or private sectors. Since the firms bid competitively for these contracts, the results should be cost savings. In fact, according to Ronald Utt, former head of the Office of Management and Budget, each job competed for resulted in a savings of $9,000 per year. Utt notes that "it's not that government workers are lazier or less capable; it's just the way that resources are managed in a monopolistic atmosphere. . . . The manager has no incentive; he or she is not in competition with anyone."[6]

The third technique is the voucher system in which the government provides purchasing power to eligible consumers. They in turn spend their vouchers on designated goods and services. Food stamps and housing vouchers for low-income families are examples. User fees and deregulation are also classified as methods of privatization.

THE COMPETITIVE MARKET

An old question that has been discussed since the development of government and debated within the United States from as early as the 1880s is whether government services should be performed by a private or a public organization. Over the course of the century the emphasis of contracting out to private sectors has both increased and decreased. Currently it is a topic of discussion across the nation.

The concept of private delivery, also known as contracting, rests on the basis of competition and the free enterprise system. A widely accepted principle is that the greatest efficiency and the lowest costs occur when there is real competition. The comparative marketplace, characterized by individual initiative and innovation, is the primary source of our national economic strength.

The first instance of a government service competing with private enterprise was in 1934, when the U.S. Navy opened its own rope factory. The rationale was that it would be more efficient to have a single government, rather than a number of private firms, provide public services. During the 1900s there was a large growth in government. While population doubled, government expenditures grew 71 times larger and the number of government employees multiplied eight times.[7]

In the mid-1930s a special committee of the U.S. House of Representatives was formed to investigate government competition. The committee recommended that, for reasons of economy, the government enter into contracts with private competitive bidders and reduce the amount of government personnel and government-purchased equipment. This emphasis continued throughout the 1950s under the Eisenhower administration, when around two thousand commercial and industrial installations operated directly by government agencies were discontinued.[8]

Today private firms are used for the delivery of services. However, according to the administrator of the Office of Federal Procurement Policy, the federal government still engages in over $20-billion worth of commercial services.[9]

A major reason for the growth of privatization are fiscal constraints under which local governments operate. Looking at privatization in 1983, as compared to 1973, the levels of privatization of specific services were two, three, five, or ten times as high as they were a decade earlier. This can be called a privatization revolution.

REASONS FOR PRIVATIZATION

Government intervention in the 1960s and 1970s brought about the concept of privatization. The public sector during this period was viewed as being the major contributor to economic growth. After numerous economic setbacks in the 1970s, the weaknesses of the public sector began to show. This caused the government's influence on and intervention in the public sector to be questioned and the discussion about and action toward privatization to occur. Private sector supporters felt that many functions performed by the government could have been better performed by the private sector. They felt this could be done directly or indirectly, or left to the marketplace. However, privatization was the answer to economic problems. This is how the privatization movement came about in 1980. It has been increasing ever since.

The privatization revolution has occurred in three stages. The first stage consisted largely of contracting out the city or county's housekeeping services, such as building maintenance, vehicle fleet management and maintenance, cutting the grass in parks, running the data processing department, and obtaining engineering services. These were relatively easy to privatize because many local firms were already providing these services to businesses and because there was nothing controversial about a city doing what businesses have always done, making make or buy decisions.

Stage 2 occurred later because it was potentially more controversial. It involved contracting out or shedding highly visible services delivered directly to the public. This included services such as garbage collection, street sweeping, emergency ambulance service, golf course operation, and even fire protection and police work. Some cities have always relied on the private sector to pick up the garbage or provide ambulance service. But what was new for the 1970s and 1980s was for cities to switch from doing these services in-house to using private enterprises.

Stage 3 is only a few years old. It involves privatization of large-scale infrastructure projects. These include waste-water treatment plants, resource recovery plants, water systems, jails and prisons, hospitals, and highways and freeways. What happens, typically, is that a consortium of an investment banking firm, a Big 8 accounting firm, and a large engineering and construction firm offers cities a package, including financing, design, construction, and operation of the facility for perhaps a twenty-year period.[10]

A consulting firm called Ecodata conducted a study in 1985 that looked at a variety of public works services in southern California. The study compared ten cities that performed each service in-house with government employees and ten comparable cities that contracted with private enterprises for each service. The results showed that for street maintenance, the government was 37 percent more costly than private enterprise, street cleaning and lawn maintenance were 43 percent more costly, traffic signal maintenance was 56 percent more costly, building maintenance was 73 percent more expensive, and asphalt paving was 96 percent more costly. The only service for which government was not more costly was payroll processing, where the public and private sector costs were the same.[11]

ARGUMENTS FOR PRIVATIZATION

Arguments for privatization include the following:[12]

1. In a public enterprise, politicians interfere with operations. Also, government intervention is a problem.

2. In a public enterprise, managers are poorly paid, poorly motivated, and inadequately monitored.

3. In public sectors, labor unions are too powerful.

All these factors have decreased the efficiency of the public sector and made the private sector even more appealing. Also, this has made public enterprises rely more heavily on budgetary support. Owners, managers, and employees of public enterprises are not as willing to meet objectives because their gains and losses are dispersed. Privatization can be a solution to these problems in public companies.

ARGUMENTS AGAINST PRIVATIZATION

Arguments against privatization include the following:[13]

1. Public enterprises serve many economic, social, and political objectives.

2. Public ownership allows government to enforce objectives which, many times, the market ignores, such as social equity, employment, and affordable goods and services.

These arguments are well taken. However, one must ask if the cost of a public enterprise is worth any of the benefits received from it. One main point remains: the majority of people are dissatisfied with public enterprises.

In *Privatizing the Public Sector*, E. S. Savas discusses privatized companies and their success. He uses the following criteria to evaluate sectors: efficiency, effectiveness, and equity.

For example, Savas notes that in the public and private airlines of Austria, certain responsibilities were required of each airline. However, the private airlines were more efficient, effective, and equitable. The costs of public bus services in the Federal Republic of Germany were 160 percent more than those of private bus services.[14] The same services were available in both the private and the public companies. The same phenomenon was evident in the education services of New York. The New York State Department of Education found that the cost of graduating from a public university was higher per student than graduating from a private university.[15] The study also found that the public schools were overstaffed. Therefore, economically and efficiently, the public schools were not satisfactory compared to the private schools. Savas found that private nursing homes had lower costs per patient than public nursing homes. Finally, public administration of health insurance was 18 to 35 percent higher per claim than private administration.[16]

Savas gives four reasons for the higher cost of public services.

1. The private sector has more competition than the public sector. Therefore, the private sector is under more pressure to be efficient.
2. The public sector is under more pressure to provide jobs than the private sector.
3. There are more incentives for private managers to produce maximum efficiency than there are for public managers. These incentives include profits and promotion.
4. There are more government regulations in the public sector which increase costs.

PUBLIC VERSUS PRIVATE

Although the major energy, transportation, and communications systems are called "public utilities," they have largely maintained private ownership in the United States. In this country privatization has come to mean mainly government reliance on private producers for services for which the government remains responsible. This is a new name for contracting.[17]

Privatization has a number of advantages. First, it promotes small business expansion because private businesses will compete for contracts from the government. The competition between various private entities will secure economic freedom and keep businesses free from centralized political control. Privatization will also increase the efficiency of operation of services and improve the delivery and quality of service. Another advantage of privatization is that it will reduce government bureaucracy by decreasing the amount of red tape involved. Private enterprises are more likely to get things done in less time.

Savas maintains that privatization means relying more on the private sector and less on the government. He believes that the private sector can provide more for the public than the government can. He asserts that privatization can reduce costs, but at the same time it can provide more efficient and effective services to the public. He also believes that state-owned enterprises (SOEs) are long overdue and become very profitable for both the business world and the public. Through privatization governments will be restored to their original role and most important purpose.

There is also opposition to privatization. Many people are concerned about the unemployment rate of government workers because of privatization. If an enterprise is privatized, many people will lose high-paying government jobs with excellent benefits. Most likely these workers will not be able to obtain a job in the private sector that pays as well. Many people will be laid off and be unable to find another job. It is for this reason that government employees and labor unions generally oppose privatization.

In other countries political and ideological considerations prevent privatization. Buyers may feel there is too much risk because privatization is a relatively new and untested concept. Politicians may fear change from their routine and see certain state companies as national symbols. A politician would not want to support a change that would have negative consequences. Another concern of government employees is that government will lose control and accountability. The government has a monopoly over the postal system, and many are not certain that the government should lose control of this and other services.

Lawrence H. Wortzel, a professor at Boston University, notes that "privatization is a worthwhile goal if it can accomplish even some of its objectives. Often, however, wholesale privatizing of state enterprises is virtually impossible to accomplish successfully. There are simply too many barriers and costs to privatization." Wortzel suggests that "private sector-style" innovation be applied. He believes that there are ways to obtain the goals of privatization without complete divesture. For example, the government might lease a state enterprise's assets to the private sector. The private sector will then use these assets to provide services produced by the state enterprise. Wortzel believes that this will be more effective than complete privatization.[18]

Private firms say privatization will offer better service at lower costs. The cost to the public would be lowered because the government would accept bids from private companies. The lowest bid would be accepted which is almost always lower than if government employees performed the service. This method also ensures that the job is done by specialists who can do the work more effectively and efficiently.

Where competition is introduced, costs will fall. So privatization should be appealing not only to business firms eager for a chance to sell to the government but also to managers frustrated by a costly and unresponsive public bureau and to citizens eager to see service made more effective without an increase in their taxes.[19]

Another government organization that has gone private is the court system. Neighborhood dispute resolution centers have emerged to quickly and inexpensively solve civil conflicts that might otherwise take years in the overburdened judicial system. Entrepreneurs are luring judges out of retirement to work in private for profit courts such as Civicourt, Inc., in Phoenix and Judicate in Philadelphia. The most popular "rent a judge" is most likely Joseph Wapner, who stars in the television program "The People's Court."[20]

Proponents of privatization argue that privately managed services are better able to meet the needs of the public through market forces. Needs are seen and immediately met by "giving power back to the people."[21]

Randall Fitzgerald points out that the United Parcel Service now controls 70 percent of the parcel delivery market, which was once part of the U.S. Postal Service's monopoly. As the Postal Service continues to lose money, entrepreneurs are eyeing the service for takeover and the U.S. Justice Department is studying the feasibility of privatizing the Postal Service.[22]

Privatization is also proposed for the nation's air traffic control system, which is currently operated by the Federal Aviation Administration. Economic deregulation of the air industry a decade ago has increased air traffic, while the firing of striking controllers reduced the number of experienced personnel in the nation's control towers.

Under one privatization proposal, the government would sell the entire corporation, which would then be free to sell stock and set market prices for airport access. Controllers would gain a share in the ownership of the private company and FAA would retain its role of overseeing safety.

The firing of 11,500 U.S. air traffic controllers on strike forced small communities to hire private companies to keep control towers operating. Farmington, New Mexico, contracted Midwest ATC Services to operate its tower at a cost of $99,000 per year while the annual cost was $287,000 under FAA operation. According to Fitzgerald, "altogether 15 towers reopened nationwide under private management and costs dropped by one third."[23]

It is possible to privatize the public role in provision of benefits and services. The government would simply withdraw from, or reduce, its role as buyer, regulator, standard setter, and decision maker. People would be on their own to decide whether to have a service and to pay for it. Since the essence of government lies in the decision about what it will provide, what it will require and buy and make available, where and when and to whom and to what standard, privatizing the provision of a service is the real form of privatization.

Government can reduce or withdraw from its provision role by introducing fees and charges for a service to continue to produce. In many cases the financing responsibility will still be shared between taxpayers and users, but the proportion paid by users will rise.

A privatization program is possible, but for the moment both private and political leaders are trapped in their old ways of thinking. Public officials are bound by traditional concepts of government that are insensitive to the need for economy and responsiveness. Private providers, on the other hand, seem unaware of the need for equity. A new concept combining equity in the provision of services with competition in production remains to be articulated politically.[24]

THE INTERNATIONAL ASPECTS OF PRIVATIZATION

Privatization has taken place in the public sector of both developed and developing countries. The term *public company* in most of the developing and some developed countries means government-owned or -controlled enterprise. In the United States the term *public* refers to those companies that trade their stocks in a public place.

Government-owned enterprises (GOEs) in less developed countries (LDCs) are considered an important tool for controlling prices and employment. Their concern is not necessarily profit maximization, but also to provide political, social, cultural, and economic stability in the country based on the ideological belief of the government and the political scheme in general.

Many developing countries have adopted ideologies which fall under the rubric of socialism. Such ideologies provide a basis for state intervention in the economy. The change of ownership from public to private is a radical departure from the goals of socialism. Such a complete rupture may be unacceptable for many developing countries which profess some form of socialism.

PRIVATIZATION IN THE UNITED STATES

In the United States, contracting out (most notable in the Defense Department) is the most common form of privatization. This is largely the result of taxpayer pressure for more efficiency. On the federal level, in addition to the Conrail sale mentioned earlier, the Department of Education and Farmers Home Administration have been involved in the sale of loans. In 1988, the Office of Management and Budget (OMB) proposed the following privatization initiatives: the sale of five power-marketing administrations, two oil fields owned by the Department of Energy, excess General Services Administration (GSA) property, Farmers Home Administration's (FHA) rural housing insurance fund, and Amtrak.

A commission was established in 1987 to review and identify programs that are not the government's responsibility or that could be performed more efficiently by private firms. On its agenda for scrutiny were low-income housing, housing finance, federal loan programs, air traffic control, educational programs, the Postal Service, operations of military commissaries and prisons, federal asset sales, and programs like Medicare and urban mass transit. In all cases, the commission felt that efficiency, quality of service, or both were likely if privatization were to take place.

PRIVATIZATION IN EUROPE

Privatization is also growing in popularity in Europe. Both conservative and socialist parties are reviving their economies by selling state-owned businesses. There is a shift of ownership from strict and rigid bureaucracies devoted to social goals to shareholders who are more interested in profits. This trend is changing Europe's views on government and business. The past postwar trend was nationalization of industry, but this is rapidly changing.

France is enthusiastic about privatization, as even the Conservative government of Premier Jacques Chirac sold $1.9-billion worth of shares in glass manufacturer Saint-Gobain. France plans to sell about 65 companies worth up to $45 billion by 1991. France also plans to sell such things as industrial companies, banks, television networks, and advertising agencies. Surprisingly, the French also intend to sell Renault, which has long been the symbol of nationalism in France, by the early 1990s.

PRIVATIZATION IN GREAT BRITAIN

Great Britain's privatization experience differs from that of the United States in that it involves mainly nationalized industries. A desire for accountability coupled with managerial autonomy is the underlying philosophy.

Great Britain has three major forms of public ownership on a national level. The first organizes industry as a department of the state controlled by a minister of the Crown. He is responsible to Parliament for day-to-day activities. The second form involves either sole or majority state shareholding in a company. The third and most important form of public ownership is the public corporation. Management is free from government supervision in daily operations, while the state controls the broader policies.

In 1979, Great Britain changed gears toward privatization. Some examples of enterprises that have been sold to the private sector include British Rail Hotels, English Channel Ferry Service, Jaguar, British Petroleum, British Aerospace, Britoil, British Telecom, British Gas, and British Airport Authority.

In addition to the companies mentioned above, more than a million previously public-owned housing units have been sold to residents. By doing this, the Thatcher administration got rid of a money-losing venture and at the same time eliminated operating subsidies. In addition, the government received income in the form of sales payments, and previously dependent government residents became independent homeowners.

Prime Minister Margaret Thatcher is especially involved in privatization. Thatcher began privatization (or denationalization as it is called in Europe) in 1979 not long after taking office. She sold British Gas for $7.9 billion, and it proved to be the largest stock offering in British history. The sale of British Gas attracted 4.5 million investors.

Great Britain has raised $23 billion by selling national utilities such as British Telecom and industrial companies such as British Aerospace. More and more entities are being sold every year. There are many examples of successful privatization in Great Britain. A classic example is the luxury car manufacturer, Jaguar. The company increased profits 142 percent from 1983, its last year as a state-owned company, to 1985. Another example of successful privatization is that of Cable and Wireless, which was once a company that managed telephone corporations in British territories. In 1986, they pulled in a profit of $422 million—four times its earning when owned by the state. Now they have expanded their business and serve countries from the United States to China.[25]

Another industry that has experienced privatization in Great Britain is the public transportation industry. Until a few years ago, National Bus was state-owned. The government owned almost 15,000 buses. They completely sold off the buses but in bits and pieces. The sales started off slow, but started gaining momentum as more and more investors saw the benefits of privatization.[26]

EVALUATION

There is some disagreement among economists as to whether Great Britain's privatization program has achieved the benefits claimed for it. Since most ventures have involved giant monopolistic public utilities, it is argued that privatization has only succeeded in placing these giant private monopolies under the same management. However, even if this proves to be the case, privatization has brought new income to the government and has drawn attention to the issue of efficiency.

There are some reasons for the differences in the progress of privatization in the United States and Europe. It seems that many more utilities are being sold in Europe than in the United States. The private industries in Europe are taking the risk involved with privatization and are getting very involved with it. One reason for this is that leaders in Europe are pushing for more privatization. The United States seems to be a little more reluctant. Investors in the United States seem to be much more aware of the disadvantages of privatization. Many scholars in the United States point out the negative aspects of privatization while most in Europe seem to praise privatization and its benefits.

AN INTERNATIONAL FOCUS

Privatization of government-owned enterprises has become the main focus of attention for organizations as USAID, the World Bank, and the International Monetary Fund (IMF). A review of the policy and practice of these multilateral institutions, however, indicates that the real objective of privatization is to change ownership of industrial property in developing countries from private to public rather than to make government enterprises profitable.

U.S. Agency for International Development (USAID)

"Privatization" was an important component of President Reagan's New Federalism and was the hallmark upon which his foreign policy was based. The purpose of New Federalism was to reduce the government's involvement in the economy.[27]

USAID is a federal agency in charge of applying the president's policy of reducing state involvement in the production of goods and services in those countries receiving U.S. assistance. USAID has made privatization in developing nations a top priority. It is working for privatization in hopes of transferring ownership and control of public property to the private sector. USAID has staff members in approximately forty countries to urge and assist local officials to divest their public sector. Their goal by the end of FY87 was to involve at least two privatization activities. Contracting out and partial divestures are accepted as short-term measures.[28]

USAID's objective in LDC privatization is not to improve the economic performance of public enterprises, but to change the ownership system. Its policy specifically prohibits the use of USAID funds for improving the performance of public enterprises such as the accounting system or management training. Sometimes USAID provides assistance to GOEs to expose the government enterprise to market forces and scheduled divestiture of the government interest. These assistance measures designed to improve the performance of GOEs must have identifiable benchmarks upon which gradual changes toward privatization can be measured.

The policy of privatization of USAID emanates from the ideological conviction that "a healthy independent private sector and secure individual economic freedom also serves as a strong base from which to ensure that the democratic institutions are brought into existence and remain free from centralized political control."[29]

The International Monetary Fund (IMF)

IMF requires that a borrower nation must first put its economic house in order before it is qualified to receive balance-of-payment adjustment loans and debt rescheduling. This has meant abolition of subsidies by the government for some consumer goods, reduction of wages, reduction of government expenditures, devaluation of local currency, and general equilibrium in demand and supply. Currently, however, privatization is a top priority on the list of demands that IMF is making on borrower nations. In the late 1970s, although IMF did not directly call for privatization, the net effect of conditionality encouraged mixed economies to go in that direction.[30] IMF has favored the private export sector to public enterprises. IMF loan programs, therefore, take resources to the private sector rather than to public enterprises hoping to generate foreign exchange in order to correct the deficit in the balance of trade.

The World Bank

In the past, the World Bank preferred to finance private manufacturing enterprises as opposed to government-owned manufacturing enterprises. However, as a result of the tremendous increase in the number of GOEs in the 1960s and early 1970s and a lack of funds to undertake large industrial projects in the public sector like mines, steel mills, fertilizer plants, and pulp and paper mills, the World Bank had to support public enterprises.

In recent years, however, the bank has come back full circle and the emphasis is now on financing private manufacturing enterprises. A. W. Clausen, the bank's president until 1986, declared that the World Bank is "partner with the private sector in the economic development of the Third World."[31] He pledged to help strengthen the private sector in LDCs by providing advice and funding. To encourage foreign direct investment flows in developing countries, the bank has taken measures to create agencies that guarantee security for foreign investment in developing countries. These measures are expected to induce Third World countries to adopt privatization policy. The granting of a loan, therefore, has become contingent upon adherence to the bank's policy.[32] It is, therefore, no accident that the most fortunate World Bank and IMF fund recipients have been the countries which have privatized the most, particularly Brazil, Mexico, and Peru.[33]

MULTINATIONAL CORPORATIONS

Multinational corporations have favored doing business with government enterprises because of political connections and tariff advantages. State enterprises in developing countries by the 1980s had become major debtors in international capital markets. The total loans dispersed to state enterprises in developing countries had reached an estimated $12.2 billion by 1978. This figure has more than doubled in recent years. This high leverage of state enterprises is indicative of the favorable attitudes banks and loan agencies have had toward state enterprises. All this has changed radically. For the first time in history, developing countries have become net exporters of capital to industrialized countries through payment of interest on their loans. The world banking community is grippled with fear of default by developing countries, which may threaten the banking system as a whole.[34] As a condition of receiving aid and loans, developing state governments have increasingly been pressured to reduce subsidy to state enterprises. Loans have been denied except to the private sector. Commercial banks have refused loans because some of the loans have been funneled to operating subsidies of the public sector.

Due to Reagan's influence the World Bank has rewritten its policy, making the granting of a loan contingent upon efforts to encourage privatization in enlisting state enterprises and strengthening the private sector. Under intense pressure from lending agencies African countries whose economies have been devastated by structural problems, falling production, exorbitant debt, payment deficits, and national calamities are forced to pay lip service to the newly enacted privatization proposal in order to receive needed loans.

THE GOVERNMENT'S ROLE

Privatization in the United States and developing countries has been increasing steadily in the past two decades. The objective of privatization is to change ownership of industrial property and services from state or federally owned to privately owned. This will keep the government from making a profit and give that opportunity to private business enterprises. By doing so there are advantages for the government, public enterprise, and the public. The government profits from the increased amount of effort that will be put into its original role of regulation. The government will be able to increase capabilities of various departments and concentrate fully on them. Public enterprise will, of course, benefit from the opportunity for profit. The public will benefit the most. There will be increased specialization because a private enterprise will be able to devote more time to a specific area of service than the government would. This will increase the quality of the product or service. While these private enterprises are competing against each other, the price of the product or service will be lowered. When separate private enterprises take the place of one large government monopoly, prices will drop. The public itself can greatly benefit from the privatization of state-owned enterprise.

Privatization must, because it is a basically new idea, be handled with great care. The government should investigate a private firm thoroughly before considering privatization. There should be a department of the government that helps with the transition from government-owned to privately owned. This department could regulate the transactions between the government and the private enterprise and act as a mediator when problems arise.

There will always be problems with any new policy or idea, and privatization is no exception to the rule. Programs can be implemented by either the government or a separate department specializing in privatization to educate those involved in the effects of privatization. Many people in the business world have misguided notions of privatization and are, therefore, afraid to experiment with it. Once people are informed of privatization and its benefits and possible obstacles, it will be much easier to overcome these obstacles.

It is unclear how profitable state enterprises will become once they are privatized. There is little evidence to show increased performance after a government-controlled enterprise is converted from state to private ownership. For example, Togo, under pressure from USAID and the World Bank, privatized a few state enterprises. Despite extensive measures to assist the private enterprises, it is still uncertain whether they will become profitable.[35]

NOTES

1. Richard Hemming and Ali M. Mansor, "Is Privatization the Answer?" *Finance and Development* (September 1988): 31.

2. Yair Aharoni, *The Evolution and Management of State Owned Enterprises* (Hagerstown, Md.: Harper and Row, 1987); U.S. Agency for International Development, *Implementing A.I.D. Privatization Objectives* (Washington, D.C., 1986).

3. Robert W. Poole, "Privatizing City Services," *Vital Speeches of the Day* (July 15, 1987): 588–90.

4. Richard C. Moe, "Exploring the Limits of Privatization," *Public Administration Review* (November–December 1987): 453.

5. Hemming and Mansor, "Is Privatization the Answer?" p. 31.

6. Murry Weidenbaum, "At the Federal Level in Particular . . . ," *Industry Week* (July 3, 1989): 56.

7. Cheryl O. Ronk, "The Growing Interest in Privatization," *USA Today* (January 1989): 30–32.

8. Ibid.

9. Ibid.

10. Poole, "Privatizing City Services," pp. 588–90.

11. Ibid.

12. Hemming and Mansor, "Is Privatization the Answer?" p. 32.

13. Ibid.

14. E. S. Savas, *Privatizing the Public Sector* (Chatham, N.J.: Chatham House, 1982), p. 96.

15. Ibid., p. 97.

16. Ibid., p. 99.

17. Ted Kilderie, "What Do We Mean by Privatization?" *Society* (September–October 1987): 46–51.

18. "Electricity Privatization," *Economist* (January 28, 1989): 56.

19. Ibid., p. 49.

20. Ibid., p. 50.

21. "Privatizing Government," *Futurist* (March–April 1989): 55–56.

22. Ibid.

23. Ibid.

24. Kilderie, "What Do We Mean by Privatization?" p. 50.

25. Shawn Tully, "Europe Goes Wild over Privatization," *Fortune* (March 2, 1987): 68–70.

26. "Changing Up," *Economist* (January 3, 1987): 38–40.

27. Mudsen Pirie and Peter Young, "Public and Private Responsibilities in Privatization: A Strategy to Promote Privatization in Developing Countries," unpublished paper, 1986.

28. U.S. Agency for International Development, *Implementing A.I.D. Privatization Objectives*.

29. Ibid.

30. Ranlam Hirschoff, "The Privatization Drive," *Africa Report* (July–August 1986): 86–92.

31. W. Clausen, *The Development Challenge of the Eighties* (Washington, D.C.: International Bank for Reconstruction and Development, 1986), p. 363.

32. Yacob Haile-Mariam and Berhanu Mengistu, "Privatization of State Owned Enterprises in Africa South of the Sahara," *The Academy of International Business Proceedings*, Southeast region, November 1987, p. 83.

33. "Privatization: Everybody's Doing It Differently," *Economist* (December 21, 1986): 71–86.

34. Harold Christopher Hune Lever, *Debt and Danger: The World Financial Crisis* (New York: Atlantic Monthly, 1986).

35. Hirschoff, "Privatization Drive," pp. 89–92.

BIBLIOGRAPHY

Goodrich, Jonathan N. "Privatization in America." *Business Horizons* (January–February 1988): 11–14.

Haile-Mariam, Yacob, and Mengistu, Berhanu. "Privatization of State Owned Enterprises in Africa South of the Sahara," *The Academy of International Business* Proceedings, Southeast region, November 1987, pp. 79–89.

Hooper, John W., et al., *The Law of Business Organizations in East and Central Africa.* Nairobi: East African Literature Bureau, 1976.

Millward, Robert. "The Comparative Performance of Public and Private Ownership." In *The Mixed Economy,* ed. E. Roll., pp. 58–93. London: Macmillan, 1982.

Modik, Stanley J. "Privatization Push to Stumble." *Industry Week* (July 3, 1989): 54–57.

"The Private Sector's New Role." *Banker's Magazine* (May–June 1989): 40.

Savas, E. S. "Private Enterprise Is Profitable Enterprise." *New York Times* (February 14, 1988): 2.

"Thatcher's New Revolution." *Business Week* (May 1, 1989): 42.

Walstedt, Bertil. *State Manufacturing Enterprise in a Mixed Economy: The Turkish Case.* Baltimore: Johns Hopkins University Press, 1980.

Wortzel, Lawrence. "Privatizing Does Not Always Work." *New York Times* (February 14, 1988): 2.

14

FUTURE PERSPECTIVES

Mergers and takeovers flourished in the 1980s and will continue to be an important factor in the future. Anyone entering the world of big business today must be aware of leveraged buyouts and "poison pills." Persons involved in both large and small businesses must be aware of takeovers.

The most pressing issues in dealing with takeovers are who is affected, what measures are being used to prevent takeover attempts, what role the government should play, and what the future is going to hold in the way of mergers and takeovers. Like major companies, large banks are very much involved in the takeover fever that has its hold on business today. The average stockholder is concerned whether the proposed buy-out will raise or lower the value of his or her shares.

There has been a tremendous amount of activity in the merger and takeover arena in the recent past. There are many reasons for this phenomenon. Management of large public companies saw that the price of their shares was undervalued. This led them to consider taking their companies private through a leveraged buyout. Another important reason for the large upswing in mergers and takeovers is the liquidity of today's markets. The vast amounts of easily available cash from commercial banks help the trend continue upward. The banks sell pieces of their loans to increase capacity and can no longer look to corporate or LDC lending as a major contributor to that liquidity. Ronald Freeman

Company, head of Salomon Brothers' merger and takeovers effort, says it is "the most important driving force" behind today's merger boom.[1]

Other important factors in the merger and acquisition rise are the junk bond market and the large investment banks of Wall Street. The junk bond market is valued at $150 million.[2] The large number of leveraged buyouts has reduced the price of the target's high-rated debt and may even encourage growth in the junk bond market. Investors are investing in the debt of a leveraged company to make sure their losses will be less if something goes wrong. Investment banks have aided the takeover boom through their leveraged buyout funds, which combine their capital with money raised from institutional investors to enable the buyouts to happen.

The most important factor in the takeover craze, however, has been the fall in the stock market. The largest companies are still very profitable, but the price of their stock is quite low. This makes these companies easy targets for corporate raiders. Raiders are willing to offer 50 to 60 percent above a company's stock market price today, as compared with 37 or 38 percent just a few years ago.[3]

The year 1988 was a historic year in the field of mergers and takeovers. There were more deals worth more money than ever before. The fifty largest transactions added up to $111.8 billion, easily surpassing the previous mark of $94.6 billion set in 1985.[4] Not included in this total was the RJR Nabisco deal, which was not yet finalized by year's end. This buyout, worth a reported $25 billion, was the largest in history.

The essence of the RJR Nabisco deal was that upper management led by Ross Johnson knew the company was undervalued. They wanted to take the company private. The management team made several offers to stockholders, the last being $108 a share. The competition for RJR Nabisco was Kohlberg, Kravis, & Roberts, a Wall Street investment firm. Their final offer to RJR stockholders was $109 a share, which was accepted. This makes Kohlberg, Kravis, & Roberts one of the largest companies in the nation.

Foreign companies were also important players in the arena of mergers and takeovers in 1988. The major reason for their interest was the cheaper dollar. The Japanese were the most successful. A major victory for the Japanese was Bridgestone's takeover of tire manufacturer Firestone, which was the largest ever American acquisition by a Japanese company. Another Japanese takeover was the purchase of CBS Records by Sony. Even though the Japanese may have been the most successful in terms of numbers, the largest foreign deal was Canadian developer Robert Campeaus' acquisition of the Federated Department Store chain.[5] According to a list compiled by *Fortune* magazine in January 1989, only one of the top ten mergers and takeovers was a leveraged buyout. The top fifty deals included only six leveraged buyouts. Most industry analysts believe there will be more leveraged buyouts in the years to come.

With all of the activity that has taken place in this area it would seem that most of the really big deals have been made. That is definitely not true. Many companies in search of growth find it cheaper to buy other companies than to develop a new business. Companies that are prime targets for takeovers have similar characteristics. Raiders are looking for companies with large stockpiles of cash, undervalued assets, poor management, or a desirable franchise. Two companies that could be targeted for takeover could be Mead Corporation and Louisiana-Pacific Corporation. Louisiana-Pacific recently collected $340 million in cash in a legal settlement with the federal government, giving it the largest bank account of any U.S. paper company. Mead Corporation is valued for its Lexis and Nexis data bases.[6]

Companies that are having hard times also tend to be targets for takeovers. An example of a company in this position would be Lotus Development Corporation. Their problem is a continual delay in introducing new products.[7] Lotus could be an attractive takeover option to another computer company or another firm in the electronic communications industry.

GOVERNMENT PLANNING

The U.S. tax code is very conducive to LBO activity because it permits investors to deduct interest on debts. This deduction decreases tax liability so that cash which would have been used to pay taxes may be used to reduce the principal of the loan.

The accounting procedure for such an acquisition of a company's assets reflects a tax savings. The value of the assets can be increased from book value to approximate market value on the acquisition date. Because this value is increased, depreciation is increased which in turn decreases the company's taxable income and tax liability.

In this instance the seller of the company also benefits. If the sale qualifies for capital gain, the seller is liable for taxes on 40 percent of the gains recognized. The leniency of the tax code permits debtors to use IOUs as tax shelters and charge part of the cost to the federal government.

Due to these facts, Congress may take action on leveraged buyouts. Cancellation or limitation of the deductibility of debt on leveraged buyouts is a possibility. President George Bush is opposed to this idea, so it probably will not be implemented. Another option is stopping the double taxation of dividends. Those who want to change the law say the double taxation encourages corporations to raise money by borrowing rather than by issuing stock. Opponents say it means less tax dollars for Uncle Sam.[8]

An interesting change would be the taxing of nonprofit organizations. Pension and other funds from organizations like Harvard University, the Salvation Army, and Massachusetts Institute of Technology were used in the RJR Nabisco leveraged buyout. These nonprofit organizations do not pay taxes on profits, but neither do they pay any interest on dividends.[9] Congress is now investigating the possibility that they might have to pay. Along with that, Congress may control or ban pension fund investments in leveraged buyouts under the Economic Research Institution and Service Association (ERISA). This is of major significance because it is estimated that pension funds now contain over $2 trillion.

Also under congressional consideration is lengthening mandatory advance notice of mergers under the Hart–Scott–Rodino Law. This would allow for a more thorough study of the proposed deal by SEC.

Antitrust laws may be strengthened in dealing with leveraged buyouts. Markets may be defined less broadly in order to limit some mergers. There could be a stricter enforcement of already existing laws to slow takeovers.

Finally, some think the states should get more involved. They feel that state laws should be made tougher to protect against unfair leveraged buyouts.[10]

As long as the government continues to provide tax advantages and little regulation of company buyouts, this trend will continue in the business sector.

Only time will tell how President Bush will handle the pressures being put upon government by those who want buyouts to remain unregulated and those who are demanding regulations.

Many argue that Congress should stay out of leveraged buyouts. Opponents of congressional intervention in the leveraged buyout area feel that regulation will give foreign companies unfair advantages. They cite the fact that the dollar is soft and foreign investors would get an extra benefit because they could deduct interest.[11]

THE FUTURE OF LEVERAGED BUYOUTS

The future of leveraged buyouts is very hard to predict at this time. One thing that will probably continue is the "poison pill" antitakeover strategy. Poison pills are things done by a company to make it extremely expensive for another firm to try a hostile takeover. A new antitakeover strategy could be "people pills." People pills are the threat that a target company's management will quit if the company is bought out.[12] This idea was first proposed by Romeo J. Ventres, CEO of Borden, Inc. First, guidelines are set for the board of directors to determine a takeover price. Second, if the company is acquired for less than what the board thinks is fair, the top twenty-five managers agree to resign. The acquiring firm must then pay the managers between $10 million and $30 million depending on the situation.[13]

There will probably be more antitakeover activity in the future, but the era of the leveraged buyout is here to stay. Large amounts of money can be made through this strategy, so it is unlikely anything will be done to limit leveraged buyouts. There are short-term drawbacks such as the loss of jobs and loss of federal tax dollars, but due to the vastness of these companies, future taxes might be greater. Though long-term effects are unclear, they will probably be positive. There is a high probability that there will be more mergers and takeovers during the 1990s.

THE 1990s

One of the largest worries of lawmakers relative to future mergers is the increase in the number of junk bonds which are distributed to cover the expenses of a takeover. These junk bonds contribute to the number of bankruptcies and make the economy more vulnerable to recession. In 1988 alone junk bonds totaled over $13 billion, bringing the total over $45 billion since 1986.

It is unlikely that the government will try to limit future mergers and corporate takeovers. They may curb tax deductions on interest on takeover debt, which discourages leveraged deals in which investors put little money down. But U.S. companies have been looked at as a bargain to overseas investors who can manufacture more cheaply in this country. In 1988, foreign investors accounted for 15 percent of the total number of takeovers and acquisitions in the United States. Great Britain alone has bought 112 American companies, and deals by foreigners made up over 20 percent of the total takeovers by 1990.

During the last few years the major target of takeover bids were consumer goods companies. Due to substantial biddings in these areas prices have been overinflated and out of reach for takeover bids. As a result of these overbiddings, the new potential takeover targets include undervalued utilities and industrial firms. Since 1982 industrial firms have slashed costs, and the weak dollar has boosted sales overseas.

NOTES

1. Nancy McConnell, "Mergers and Acquisitions," *Fortune* (January 2, 1989).
2. Ibid.

3. Ibid.
4. Ronald Henkoff, "Deals of the Year," *Fortune* (January 30, 1989): 162–70.
5. Ibid.
6. Jon Friedman, "Takeover Stocks: No, the Good Ones Aren't All Taken," *Business Week* (December 26, 1988): 110, 114.
7. Ibid.
8. Shirley Hobbs Scheibla, "K.O. L.B.O.'s? Congress Turns a Cold Eye on Buyouts," *Barron's* (December 19, 1988).
9. Ibid.
10. Ibid.
11. "Takeovers: Congress Should Butt Out," *Business Week* (December 19, 1988): 118.
12. Christopher Farrell, "First It Was Poison Pills—Now It's People Pills," *Business Week* (January 16, 1989): 33–34.
13. Ibid.

BIBLIOGRAPHY

Farrell, Christopher. "First It Was Poison Pills—Now It's People Pills." *Business Week* (January 16, 1989): 33–34.
Friedman, Jon. "Takeover Stocks: No, the Good Ones Aren't All Taken." *Business Week* (December 26, 1988): 110, 114.
Henkoff, Ronald. "Deals of the Year." *Fortune* (January 30, 1989): 162–170.
McConnell, Nancy. "Mergers and Acquisitions." *Fortune* (January 2, 1989).
Scheibla, Shirley Hobbs. "K.O. L.B.O.'s? Congress Turns a Cold Eye on Buyouts." *Barron's* (December 19, 1988): 15, 59.
"Takeovers: Congress Should Butt Out." *Business Week* (December 19, 1988): 118.

15

MANAGERIAL PERSPECTIVES

Mergers and acquisitions have affected the business community for years. Various experts are concerned with these effects and the best course of action to take in an acquisition.

Murphy Lawes is concerned with the undermining of equity in the corporate world.[1] He believes that banks are acting irresponsibly in their pursuit of acquisitions to expand the figures on the balance sheet. Banks are able to lend massive amounts of money because there has been a low rate of loan defaults. Lawes maintains that managers become more productive because they have a direct interest in the survival of the company. This is important because the survival of lending institutions and the productivity of manager-owned companies are necessary to the survival of American business.[2]

Brett D. Fromson believes that takeovers and acquisitions can increase the profitability of a corporation in the long run. Companies undergoing the acquisition process need to communicate and streamline operations to be successful. Companies have been constantly increasing the size of operations which in turn increases the total scope of the company's problems. These ideas are significant because they allow a business to survive the acquisition process. This foundation provides an environment in which the manager can expand his or her ideas.[3]

Robert J. Samuelson provides a contrasting viewpoint. He suggests that the process of takeovers and acquisitions exemplifies the basic greed of American society and will prevent the establishment of new small businesses. Small businesses can thrive, however, by being acquired by a larger company. The parent corporation can provide sufficient capital to allow the subsidiary company to expand.[4]

Peter F. Drucker feels that takeovers may be the reason that America is not as competitive as it was in the past. He also believes that America is losing its technology leadership. As a result, he feels that mergers, acquisitions, and takeovers demand front-page news coverage. They affect everyone and should not be buried in a newspaper's financial page. The new competitive environment has made established corporations vulnerable to hostile takeovers. Drucker gives three reasons for this. First, inflation has distorted the value of assets and their earning power. Second, there have been many structural changes over the years. Companies are being forced to split up in order to satisfy shareholder objectives: some want long-term growth and others want present earnings. Third, Drucker feels that management has become too powerful. It is no longer monitored by its board of directors or is responsible to its shareholders. The significance of these changes is directly related to the future competitive ability of American corporations.[5]

Paul M. Hirsch of the University of Chicago has studied the changes a target corporation endures. He puts them in three categories. First, targets are fighting back. Second, targets are no longer small corporations; they now include blue-chip corporations. As a result, everyone can play the takeover game. Third, takeovers are now considered normal events. They are no longer the exception to the rule. The threat of a takeover has become routine. As a result, there is a significant change in strategies being used by targets, raiders, and managers in all corporations.[6]

Nigel Holloway in Tokyo, however, believes that Japanese firms do not consider the threat of a takeover to be the norm in Japan. When a Japanese corporation considers a takeover, they do not consider Japanese corporations. Holloway believes this is because lifetime employment makes it too hard for corporations to merge. However, Holloway admits that once the financing of takeovers becomes international, there will be more similarities in all corporations. As a result, the Japanese who believe that these types of transaction will never happen in Japan will eventually have to compete while being a possible takeover.target.[7]

STRATEGIC ALTERNATIVES

As a corporation reviews its present position in the marketplace, it has various strategic options depending upon where the corporation wants to go. These options will be studied and chosen at the highest

Figure 15.1
Corporate Strategic Options

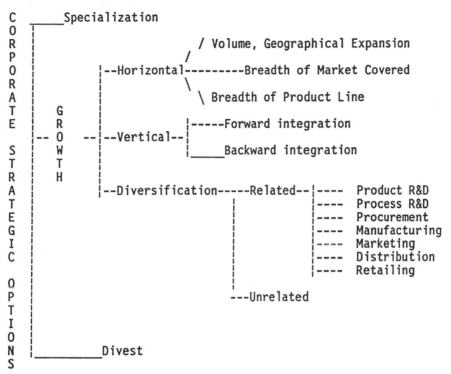

```
C       Specialization
O   
R                            / Volume, Geographical Expansion
P                           /
O            |--Horizontal---------Breadth of Market Covered
R            |               \
A            |                \ Breadth of Product Line
T     G      |
E     R      |               |-----Forward integration
      O   -- |--Vertical--|
S     W      |               |____Backward integration
T     T      |
R     H      |
A            |--Diversification-----Related--|---- Product R&D
T            |                       |       |---- Process R&D
E            |                       |       |---- Procurement
G            |                       |       |---- Manufacturing
I            |                       |       |---- Marketing
C            |                       |       |---- Distribution
             |                       |       |---- Retailing
O            |                       |
P            |                    ---Unrelated
T            |
I            |
O            |
N            |_____Divest
S
```

level of the corporation. There are mainly three strategic options the company might choose to adopt: specialization, growth, or divestment. For each of these options, high corporate level management must determine the rate of return, growth, and cost of capital potential. They will then select the option which is seen as the most viable and will yield the highest degree of profitability. Once a corporation has developed and introduced a successful product, it will begin to review its alternatives for growth and diversification (see fig. 15.1).

The first strategy a company might choose is to specialize in one product/service or related products/services (sometimes called a single business focus). Any firm which markets a related set of products or services is usually referred to as a specialized company. Most of the fast food, soft drink, and beer companies are considered to have a single business focus. Companies might specialize in a specific geographical area, channel of distribution, market segment, or choice of media.

The second strategy is growth and diversification. Most American companies expanded from one product or service to multiple products or services. Growth can be in the related area or unrelated. It can also be horizontal or vertical.

Horizontal growth looks to expand the existing business within its current product-market structure. A corporation can further increase its sales volume by penetrating both domestically and internationally.

There are two types of vertical growth: forward integration, which leads the firm closer to its customers and secures more control on their channels of distribution; and backward integration, which leads the firm closer to its raw material suppliers.

Diversification can be attained through internal development or acquisition. Acquisition is obviously the most advantageous. It is rapid and it has the advantage of facilitating accessibility to skill and competency not available internally to the firm. Diversification may include related or unrelated industries.

The third strategic option available to businesses is to divest. A company may decide to liquidate its entire operations and sell off its assets. A spinoff occurs when a company sells one or more of its strategic business units (SBU). A third type of divestment occurs when the company simply decides to reduce its production capacity over an extended period of time.

BARRIERS

If a corporation decides to enter a mature industry, it must recognize the difficulties it will encounter. The corporation will be facing competitive norms. Moreover, entry barriers, key determinants which indicate the degree of attractiveness of a particular industry, are usually very high. Before a corporation decides to enter a mature industry, it must have full knowledge of all existing barriers and a significant amount of capital. A corporation which undertakes the necessary research of entry barriers not only penetrates successfully but can also prevent penetration of new and larger firms.

Entry barriers are those forces which discourage or prevent firms from investing in a particular industry that appears attractive because of its profitability.[8] Industries known to have high entry barriers are considered to be more profitable in the long run. They become favorite targets of large firms or foreign entrants.[9]

The absence of high entry barriers would impede plant expansion. If this were to happen, supply would flood demand and prices would drop. This would force some firms to close or sell out. Plant expansions are high entry barriers because of the high cost of building and equipment. Other unattractive barriers include high exit barriers, a fragmented structure of nonhomogeneous firms, and commodity-like product traits.

All of these reduce an industry's profitability potential. The steel industry has suffered from all of these barriers. Steel companies are stuck with obsolete equipment which they cannot sell. The steel industry cannot compete with firms in the Far East because they have more advanced technology, understand the international market, and have better access to less expensive raw materials.

Industries with slow growth, predictable demand, and recognized products are called mature industries. New firms trying to obtain a niche in the market will find it harder to enter such mature industries. However, there are market segments which are easier to enter but are generally less attractive. The most successful strategic groups are called core competitors. They usually have enough market power to influence prices. An example of a core competitor is the Organization of Petroleum Exporting Countries (OPEC). During the 1970s OPEC raised the price of crude oil uniformly and the rest of the world had no other choice but to pay the price.

Late entrants to a mature industry can survive only if they have large amounts of capital or innovations. A more advanced technology, newer products, and a labor-intensive system can give late entrants a decided advantage. However, if new entrants are faced with the high costs of building a physical plant, purchasing equipment, and undertaking research and development, they are already millions of dollars behind.

Vertical integration can provide a short-term competitive edge. However, when a firm adopts a vertically integrative strategy, it risks losing strategic flexibility to adapt to changes in industry and technology. In the early 1900s, the Ford Motor Company owned and operated all stages of production. Originally, Ford had approached suppliers for support of his "horseless carriage" and was met with an industry-wide pessimism toward his radically new idea. If he had been wrong, only Ford would have suffered. Ford's vertical strategy proved successful, however, and set industry standards, lowered operating costs, and provided some form of stabilization in a turbulent business environment.[10]

Vertical integration can be downstream or upstream. Downstream integration involves relationships between entire units who act as either buyers for the product or distributors on either the wholesale or retail level. The General Electric Company is a leading producer of a silicon sealer used in the glazing industry. In the 1970s, their marketing activities within the United States reached 75 percent. The sealants are sold through an independent distributor. General Electric attempted to introduce a vertically integrative strategy by limiting the distributor of the sealant from selling a competitor's brand.[11] Most downstream integrative strategies involve full ownership of a distributional unit by the parent corporation. The Tandy/Radio Shack Company owns and operates all retail outlets for its personal computers. By dominating the distributional channel, General Electric sought to control a downstream linkage without full ownership of that business.

Upstream relationships are formed between a corporation which owns and operates a producer of raw or semiprocessed materials, components, or services. Henry Ford established an upstream relationship with the business units that provided the iron and steel for the Model T.

Before a decision to vertically integrate is made, a business must consider the dimensions of the proposed strategy. In this case, strategic dimensions are formed by the number of stages of the integrative activity, the breadth per SBUs of the activity, the degree of internal transfers, and the form of ownership required by the vertical integration.

The number of stages of the integrative activity refers to the number of steps of the production, marketing, and distributive processes that the parent firm is involved in. The firm takes ultraraw materials product components, produces a finished product, and markets and distributes it in the marketplace.[12]

Ronald Coase and Peter Williamson investigated the question of when and if a firm should adopt a vertically integrated system and found it economically beneficial for a firm to involve itself in upstream and downstream activities when the costs of transacting over markets is higher than internal management costs.[13] When there is a lack of source supply or product demand at a particular stage of production, for example, the firm should look into the possibilities of buying that stage. Another aspect which must be considered to make strategic decisions to integrate vertically is the specificity of each transaction. When transactions involve a flow of economies, such as the physical proximity of a production plant between stages, they are positively related to vertical integration.[14]

Advertising is also a transaction-specific cost and is positively related to vertical integration. A transaction-specific investment such as advertising is needed when the production process involves nonstandardized products. A company tends to advertise a new and different product to establish initial market demand or when entering an existing mature market. Human capital is considered a transaction-specific cost when there is a great importance placed on research and development activities. When the cost of human resources increases, technologically dependent firms will be attracted to vertical integration.

CHARACTERISTICS OF TARGET COMPANIES

A corporation subject to a takeover or buyout is usually a mature, cash-rich company. Furthermore, it is usually experiencing little growth. The corporation has very little risk associated with it, especially to lending institutions that are involved in the LBO business. According to the

Boston Consulting Group (BCG) Matrix, if a company is mature and experiencing low growth, it should either diversify or divest some of the "dog" product lines. Therefore, a good management team with long-term strategies milks its cash cows and pumps the money into its question marks. Good management uses this established cash flow, instead of lowering its debt to equity ratio, to create long-term growth.

The long-term goal of stockholders is to make a profit. An investor in a mature company is afraid of risk. Consequently, he would not want to pay a lot of greenmail. It is usually the management that wants to pay the greenmail to keep their jobs. To battle a takeover when stock prices are surging only makes sense to management and the board of directors. The corporation should take on a higher debt-to-equity ratio in order to grow; however, a poison pill is not the "reactive" answer. The conservative investor did not have this as a long-term goal and cannot accept the risk.

There are many mature, cash-rich corporations that are not long term-oriented. This is due to the "don't rock the boat" syndrome of managers and BODs.[15] Many corporations have become content with marginal earnings. Perhaps this is the self-fulfilling prophecy of a corporation when it becomes huge and bureaucratic. LBOs and corporate raiders are a necessary evil to get companies to "trim-the-fat." This will lead to value maximization of the corporation instead of a leisurely "stroll in the park." And in return, more highly focused long-term goals will evolve, making the large, mature corporations of the United States more competitive worldwide.

AN ACCOUNTING PERSPECTIVE

In pooling accounting, the balance sheets and income statement are combined to form a new company. In purchasing accounting, the balance sheet and income statement of one company are added to that of the other company. This is done at requisition value, not at book value.[16] The first accounting motive is tax advantageous. One advantage would be that the taxation of dividends, which would have occurred if all earnings were distributed, is avoided. A corporation is allowed to carry forward corporate tax losses and use these losses to offset future income. If a corporation has too high of a loss to carry forward and low future income prospects, the corporation may not utilize all of the loss carryover. Therefore, there can be a tax benefit when acquiring a profit-earning corporation or being acquired by one. Another accounting motive is to gain promotional profits. The advantages apply to a corporation with low profit income; they combine these marginal profits with another corporation's profits to lower total combined profits. In turn, taxes may be lowered.

A company needs to have a structured plan in order to sell or buy a corporation. Before the actual transaction of an M&A takes place, a decision must be made to determine which corporation should survive. The plan must recognize which of the corporations has the most favorable certificate of incorporation. A detailed M&A contract should be drafted. This contract should include the relationship between pension, profit sharing, stock option, and other fringe benefit plans of the buyer and seller. A corporation and its stockholders want to clarify the buying corporation's plans for the employees' benefits and stockholders' options. This should be done prior to the M&A.

Another factor that needs to be considered in an M&A structured plan is bank loan agreements. The acquirer should be aware of the acquiree's current loans; the acquirer may want to refinance the existing debt. This may seem to be a minor detail; however, in actuality it would cause greater problems later if not clarified before the M&A is completed. The final factor is the pooling of interests from an accounting point of view. There is usually an intangible asset that can be acquired—goodwill. In order for this to be acquired, the M&A must be treated as a pooling of interests. Depending on circumstances, goodwill can be added or written off.

There are a few defensive maneuvers a corporation can use for M&As. Management should establish procedural safeguards to alert itself to any initial stirrings of an M&A. Management should work closely with the specialists handling the corporation's stock to keep an eye on any trading developments. A company also needs to examine the laws that may form the foundation of litigation to prohibit or hinder an M&A. If the corporation does its research properly it will be able to detect bidders' improper moves. The government has enacted laws and rules to control some M&As to restrict the takeovers. These laws help control how far a corporation can go during an M&A. Most laws protect the target corporation.

What does the future hold for businesses in terms of M&As? New accounting policies may be adopted under SEC. New jobs may be created because additional financial accounting staff will be needed to meet corporate requirements. Corporate executives may be required to do more research in order to obtain experience in the field of M&As. A company may require more work time for management to allow for modification and precautionary measures.

MANAGEMENT BEFORE RESTRUCTURING

In order to understand the typical type of management that exists before a merger and acquisition (M&A), a trend must be discussed. This trend is the change in corporate governance that was described as far back as 1932 by Adolf Berle and Gerdiner Means. The property rights associated with stock ownership no longer give stockholders control over their property. Berle and Means attribute this to four factors. First, share ownership of most corporations is widely dispersed throughout society. Second, owners of large corporations do not have control over corporation resources. Third, individual stockholders have little power to effect change. Finally, small stockholders see themselves as investors rather than owners of corporations.[17] Drucker refers to this type of management as "corporate capitalism." In this scenario, managers act as if they are the owners of the corporation and feel that they do not fall under the control of the BOD.

This type of management is typical before a takeover; there is no stockholder or stakeholder loyalty. This, however, falls just short of Karl Marx's belief that capitalists will devour each other. Stockholders often support a takeover by selling their shares at a high price for individual short-term gains. Many shareholders support a takeover in the false belief that it will result in restructuring that will employ a more efficient use of resources. This is not true because the most valuable aspects of the acquired business are usually sold after a hostile takeover in order to pay off the huge debt that financed the takeover. This impairs the productivity of the corporation. In a nutshell, this leads to the conclusion that a hostile takeover is only a symptom of corporate capitalism.

LAST TACTIC BEFORE THE BID

Prior to an M&A offer, management can sign a standstill agreement. This is a last effort, and it is no longer a proactive approach to management. When managers feel that their corporation is a takeover target, they give information about their corporation to corporations that are expected to make such an attempt. They are now obligated not to make a takeover attempt by buying shares of the corporation. The concept is that a future takeover attempt will be based on substantially more improved information.[18] This is the result of a loophole in America's Security Act. In return, management now has some time to try to win over a majority of the shareholders. This is management's acknowledgment that the shareholders are really the owners; however, the shareholders are not informed about the agreement. This has become a standard procedure prior to an actual takeover bid.[19] As one might guess, there is a thin line between this and inside information.

In its most simplified form, an M&A has three steps: offer, decisions and/or actions, and outcome. When an offer is made, management must decide whether to accept or reject it. This is the aspect of an M&A that is deemed newsworthy. The stock market reflects the surge in price even though the value of the corporation has not changed. However, there is a tendency to measure a corporation by its dividends and capital gains. Consequently, it is not hard news if management, the BOD, and stockholders are in agreement and accept the bid. However, this is usually the result of an invited M&A.

THE ACQUISITION PROCESS

During the acquisition process, the acquiring company must take several steps. First, the acquiring company must establish its long-term corporate goals. Second, the acquiring company must develop specific criteria for the acquisition. Next, the company needs to develop an acquisition and finance group. Targets need to be selected and evaluated. Finally, the acquiring company must assimilate and evaluate the acquired company.

The development of corporate objectives and goals is the first stage in the process of merging firms. This stage requires a complete analysis of the buyer. It must be determined if the capital is available to finance the merger. Also, the company's current competitive position must be determined and projected into the future. The direction for expansion must be decided, and a detailed description of the firm the company wishes to acquire must be provided. Finally, these objectives need to be communicated to all executives, staff, and outside consultants. The CEO is responsible for setting the corporate objectives, having them approved, and communicating them throughout the company.

Next, the corporation must develop its acquisition criteria. These criteria can be classified as either broad or narrow. Examples of broad criteria include looking for a company in a particular industry; having a predetermined geographic area in which candidates should be located; making sure the acquirer's strengths will complement the candidate's weaknesses; determining the size of the company to be acquired; making sure the company is not dependent on one customer; recognizing the potential for growth; and ensuring the personnel of the acquiring firm and the firm to be acquired are compatible. The narrow criteria are financial in nature and are applied after a candidate is chosen. For example, investment must produce a minimum return on capital and the company needs to have a minimum return on sales. This criteria must be followed exactly by the searching company in order for the acquisition to be successful.

The actual acquisition team is then set up. The team may be a corporate group or a corporate group with an acquisition department. Corporate groups are composed of various senior executives, including the CEO. The members interact closely and make use of a support group if necessary. In corporate groups with an acquisition department, the vice-president of corporate development is in charge of the acquisition department. The vice-president has a full-time staff to fulfill many of the steps in the process and reports to and is part of the corporate group. Both groups consist of experts from departments such as marketing, finance, and operations.

During the fourth stage, the firm must decide what type of financing is most appropriate for the particular acquisition. The preferred method of financing depends largely on the condition of the economy at the time of the acquisition. Sometimes the form of payment is decided upon during negotiation between the firms. The form of payment may be through the use of stock, debentures, cash, notes, bonds, real estate, or any combination of these.

Finally, the actual search for an acquisition candidate begins. In the passive approach the company sits back and waits for an opportunity to present itself; no actual search is done. In the active approach, a full-time acquisition department goes out and actually seeks potential candidates for a merger. There are several ways a firm may actively search for a candidate. Media advertising is extensively used. The firm searching for a candidate may put an advertisement in a journal which is published in a select geographic region. Advertisements are also placed in trade publications. Individuals outside the firm may be called upon to help in the search, such as professional brokers, business and management consultants, accountants and attorneys, commercial banks, and investment and stockbrokers. Other methods of active search include direct contact, mailings, recommendations from friends, business associates, professional acquaintances, and trade shows.

After identifying prospective candidates, the acquiring company makes a complete evaluation. When a public company is being acquired, extensive information is available from public sources, such as SEC. Information about private companies is available from the company itself and its shareholders. An extensive in-depth analysis of private firms is almost always conducted. There are three steps in the analysis of a private company: (1) the company must determine if it wants to own the other; (2) the company uses information that is available to try to get the prospective candidate to enter a nonbinding letter of intent; and (3) after signing the nonbinding letter, a purchase investment is completed. The principal goal of this evaluation is to determine if the prospective candidate meets the acquirer's criteria and to establish a price to be offered.[20] The acquiring company should make a comparison between prospective candidates, between the candidate and the acquiring firm, and between the advantages and disadvantages of the acquisition. An analysis of the financial statements should also be completed. An analysis of production, marketing, sales, management and personnel, industry and competitive position, and potential liabilities should be made. The reason the firm is available for acquisition must be determined. For example, a firm may decide to go along with a merger due to potential obsolescence of a product; it may be involved in a declining industry; or it may have a limited scope.

After finding a company which is a good acquisition candidate, the actual negotiation stage begins. Proceeding to this stage of the process requires senior-level approval. The person doing the negotiating should be the person who has the strongest personal relations with the candidates and has the strongest negotiating skills. The following are some helpful hints for maintaining trust during negotiations: (1) do not intimidate the CEO of the candidate firm; (2) establish a reputation for treating employees of acquired companies well; (3) avoid bidding matches with other companies wishing to acquire the same company; (4) do not make a process more difficult with unnecessary paperwork and delays; and (5) avoid trivial matters.[21]

The final two steps of the acquisition process are combining the two companies and conducting a postacquisition review. Included in the combining of the firms are integration of employees and management, elimination of work duplication, division of responsibility, and procedures and controls. Usually compromises must be made during the combining of the two firms. The postacquisition review is an ongoing process of keeping up with how the resulting company is doing. This can be done by reviewing recent financial statements, holding meetings of managers and employers, and examining the overall operations of the firms following the merger.

MANAGEMENT'S REACTION TO THE TAKEOVER BID

There are many ways in which management can combat a takeover. Management must pay more attention to stockholders. In turn, there will be improved voting support in a proxy fight. The corporation can also defend itself by restructuring through a leveraged buyout. This is simply taking the corporation private. As a result, management will retain full control though there is an increase in debt. This debt is self-imposed; this is acceptable in that there will be no plans of divestments simply to reduce debt. Debt is not attractive to M&As. Therefore, it is used as a defense. "Poison pills" in the forms of "golden parachutes" and "tin parachutes" protect top executives and lower-level employees if an M&A is completed. Top executives have received up to two and one-half years of compensation if they quit or get fired after an M&A.[22] Another strategy is for management to find a "white knight." A white knight is someone management feels will keep the management and the corporation intact. However, the white knight must pay even more for the corporation's shares.[23]

FINANCING MERGERS AND ACQUISITIONS

In today's business world M&As have become a fact of life. M&As have been increasing in frequency to the point where a company has to make sure it can acquire another firm if necessary. The company needs to know what institutions provide loan services. Also, the company needs to be able to negotiate the terms of the loan. Finally, the company will have to determine the amount of risk it wants to be responsible for while assuming the loan.

In 1988 bankers supplied approximately $100 billion to finance M&As. When large amounts of money such as this exchange hands, the people involved must know what they are doing. Monies which are used for M&As come from a variety of sources such as foreign banks and investors, private U.S. investors, and insurers and pension funds. Each of these sources can provide a wealth of money or a wealth of headaches.

The largest investors have been foreign investors. These include large Japanese banks and corporations who want to expand their control in the American market. The Japanese have reaped huge profits by lending large amounts of capital to U.S. firms. Also, these Japanese firms have started buying the interests of many American assets for themselves. However, these large firms are starting to realize that the M&A "mania" cannot last forever.

Also included in the group of large investors are pension funds. These funds are a collection of money from pensions, money markets, and bond funds. These funds are directed by pension managers who can influence the economy much more than the individual investor.[24] Most of the companies using a pension fund as a source of money will receive a limited amount because of the responsibility which pension fund managers have to their creditors. Pension funds tend to be conservative in their lending of money.

Recently firms in the process of an M&A would consider the junk bond as a source of money. A junk bond is a bond which returns a high yield unless the company encounters financial problems. When this occurs the junk bonds are refused payment by the issuing corporation. The junk bond was increasing in popularity until the RJR Nabisco deal, which decreased the usefulness of junk bonds because investors, attracted by the large return on investment, did not consider the risk involved. Since many of the bonds lost their value, it has become harder to attract investors.

The corporation which has considered the M&A process will have taken into consideration all the financial variables. It will have decided which financial tool will most benefit the goals of the company. The company also has to determine the amount of restructuring it will have to undergo because of the new financial burden. Some companies will have to sell less profitable divisions and concentrate their resources on the more profitable divisions. Finally, the rate of M&As will probably not decline in the near future unless the economy takes a downturn.

MANAGEMENT AND THE RESTRUCTURED CORPORATION

The outcome of a hostile takeover is usually profitable for the acquirer and chaos for management and other stakeholders. Though management may try to accept the situation graciously, many top executives may be fired. This invariably leads to low morale. Managers are also directly or indirectly affected by divestment of assets. This is the only quick way to get rid of the huge debt that was taken on when financing the M&A. Finally, the management is forced to come to terms with a new corporation with a short-term mentality. There are, however, positive aspects of a takeover, especially a friendly and invited M&A. Generally, a takeover results in short-term profits for shareholders. In a friendly M&A, a corporation can benefit from sales synergy, operating synergy, management synergy, and technology synergy.[25]

EFFECTS OF MERGERS AND ACQUISITIONS ON RESEARCH AND DEVELOPMENT

Research and development (R&D) provides the necessary innovations to keep a corporation profitable. Many experts and the government are worried that the increased load of debt from M&As has encouraged cuts in R&D. This subject has become more relevant because of increased competition from foreign corporations. However, the effects of M&As on R&D are mixed and researchers are unsure of the direct effects. Finally, some CEOs believe the problems of R&D cuts are irrelevant because most companies that are taken over are not in the high-tech or research industries.

Research and development which has been done by private companies produces products which make the consumer's life easier. Also, it provides the basis for companies to increase profits by expanding market share. Most R&D can be traced to government projects which provide the basis for products in the open market. Foreign competition has been steadily increasing their R&D budgets while U.S. companies have been steadily decreasing theirs. This development has increased the fears of many economists. They believe cuts in R&D will result in more heavy industry being lost to foreign competition.

There are two reasons for cuts in R&D. First, there have been declining revenues in the industrial sector because of foreign competition. R&D uses discretionary capital for its funding, which allows for budget reduction. Second, after an M&A occurs a corporation is saddled with a large debt. The company now has to decrease expenses in order to pay back the loan.

The National Science Foundation has concluded that companies not involved in M&As or restructuring have increased their spending by 5.4 percent while those involved in M&As decreased R&D by 5.3 percent. Finally, those companies which have undergone LBOs or restructuring have decreased R&D by 12.8 percent. These results are inconclusive, however, because the sample size was insignificant.[26]

The effects of M&As on R&D budgets cannot be readily identified because of the limited number of companies involved in R&D. Companies involved in R&D and M&As cannot be used as an example because this phenomenon is so recent. No direct conclusions can be drawn because the results could change dramatically should an economic downturn occur. Furthermore, decreasing R&D budgets can be attributed to factors other than M&As. Managers must watch for the future effects of M&As on R&D, because detrimental results might become more evident in the future.

CONCLUSION

In conclusion, management will, in the long run, protect its own best interests by protecting the basic rights that belong to the shareholders, the voters and owners of the corporation. As a result, it will have the support that is needed to achieve a conducive environment where long-term strategies can be implemented. Furthermore, the going concern of the corporation will be less emphasized with value maximization taking top priority.

NOTES

1. Murphy Lawes, "Are LBO Banks about to Crash?" *Bankers Monthly* 106 (April 1989): 24–28.

2. Ibid.

3. Bret Duval Fromson, "Life after Debt: How LBOs Do It," *Fortune* 119 (March 1989): 91–92.

4. Robert J. Samuelson, "The Irony of Capitalism," *Newsweek* (January 9, 1989): 44.

5. Peter F. Drucker, "Corporate Takeovers—What Is to Be Done?" *Public Interest* 82 (Winter 1986): 3–23.

6. Paul M. Hirsch, "From Ambushes to Golden Parachutes: Corporate Takeovers as an Instance of Cultural Framing and Institution Integration," *American Journal of Sociology* 91 (January 1986): 801–3.

7. Nigel Holloway, "Japanese Managers Changing Attitudes to Takeovers: Corporate Flirtations," *Far Eastern Economic Review* (January 26, 1989): 72.

8. Kathryn R. Harrigan, *Strategic Flexibility* (Lexington, Mass.: Lexington Books, 1985), p. 12.

9. Ibid.

10. Ibid., p. 69.

11. William S. Comanor and H. E. Frech, III, "The Competitive Effects of Vertical Agreements?" *American Economic Review* (June 1985): 544.

12. Harrigan, *Strategic Flexibility*, p. 73.

13. David T. Levy, "The Transactions Cost Approach to Vertical Integration: An Empirical Examination," *Review of Economics and Statistics* (August 1985): 439.

14. Comanor and Frech, "Competitive Effects," p. 547.

15. Sherman P. Stratford, "Pushing Corporate Boards to Be Better," *Managing* 118 (July 1988): 60.

16. Peter O. Steiner, *Mergers* (Ann Arbor: University of Michigan Press, 1975), p. 80.

17. Abbass F. Alkhafaji, *A Stakeholder Approach to Corporate Governance: Managing in a Dynamic Environment* (New York: Quorum, 1989), p. 51.

18. "Stubbed Out: Takeovers in America," *Economist* 301 (December 1986): 79.

19. Ibid.

20. Gordon Woods, "The Acquisition Decision," National Association of Accountants (Montvale, N.J. 1985): 29.

21. Ibid., p. 33.

22. Alkhafaji, *Stakeholder Approach to Corporate Governance*, p. 236.

23. Drucker, "Corporate Takeovers," p. 4.

24. Vivian Brownstein, "Where All the Money Comes from," *Fortune* 119 (January 2, 1989).

25. Thomas L. Wheelen, *Strategic Management and Business Policy* (New York: Addison-Wesley, 1986), p. 174.

26. Kathleen Deveny, "Progress Isn't Drowning in Debt—Yet," *Business Week*, Special Issue (1989): 110.

BIBLIOGRAPHY

Comanor, William S., and H. E. Frech, III. "The Competitive Effects of Vertical Agreements?" *American Economic Review* (June 1985).

Harrigan, Kathryn R. *Strategic Flexibility*. Lexington, Mass.: Lexington Books, 1985.

Hax, Arnoldo, and Nicolas Majluf. *Strategic Management: An Integrative Perspective*. Engelwood Cliffs, N.J.: Prentice-Hall, 1984.

Levy, David T. "The Transaction Cost Approach to Vertical Integration: An Empirical Examination." *Review of Economics and Statistics* (August 1985).

Perry, Martin K., and Robert H. Groff. "Resale Price Maintenance and Forward Integration into a Monopolistically Competitive Industry." *Quarterly Journal of Economics* (November 1985).

SELECT BIBLIOGRAPHY

JOURNALS

Adams, John. "Do Mergers Really Work?" *Business Week* (June 3, 1985): 88.

Agrawal, Anup, and Gershon N. Mandelker. "Managerial Incentives and Corporate Investments and Financing Decisions." *Journal of Finance* 42/4 (September 1987): 823–37.

Andrews, Kenneth R. "Rigid Rules Will Not Make a Good Board." *Harvard Business Review* (November–December 1982): 34–35.

Bandow, Doug. "Are Hostile Takeovers Good for the Economy?" *Business and Society Review* (Fall 1987): 47.

Barney, Jay B., Lowell Busenitz, James O. Fiet, and Doug Moesel. "The Structure of Venture Capital Governance: An Organizational Economic Analysis of Relations Between Venture Capital Firms and New Ventures." *Academy of Management Proceedings* (1989): 64–68.

Beck, Gordon. "When Managers Are Owners." *Time* (November 7, 1988): 99–100.

Berger, Joan, and Norman Jonas. "Do These Deals Help or Hurt the United States Economy?" *Business Week* (November 24, 1986): 86.

Berney, Karen. "A Rosen by any Other Name." *Nation's Business* (May 1988): 45.

Berry, John. "Any Deal Is Double." *Mergers & Acquisitions* (June 1988): 56.

Billingham, Carol J. "Hostile Corporate Takeovers: Why and How Their Numbers Grow." *Mid-American Journal of Business* (March 1987): 4–8.

Block, Stanley B. "Buy-Sell Agreements for Privately Held Corporations." *Journal of Accountancy* (September 1985): 114.

Blum, Stephen B. "Mergers and Acquisitions: Dealing with Intermediaries." *Management Accounting* (October 1989): 22–26.

Brown, Ann. "Merger Ethics." *Forbes* (November 4, 1985): 25.

Brownstein, Vivian. "Where All the Money Comes from." *Fortune* 119 (January 2, 1989).

Bruck, Connie. "The Old Boy and the New Boys." *New Yorker* (May 8, 1989): 81–82.

Bulvony, Matt. "Making Money—and History—at Weirton." *Business Week* (November 12, 1984): 136.

Burrough, Brian. "Takeover Boom Is Expected to Continue after a Strong First Half." *Wall Street Journal* (July 5, 1988).

Cole, Diane. "The Entrepreneurial Self." *Psychology Today* (June 1989): 60–63.

Comanor, William S., and H. E. Frech, III. "The Competitive Effects of Vertical Agreements?" *American Economic Review* (June 1985): 544.

Cook, Dan. "Thinking of Using an ESOP to Buy Your Company? Think Again." *Business Week* (August 26, 1985): 34.

Deveny, Kathleen. "Progress Isn't Drowning in Debt—Yet." *Business Week*, Special Issue (1989): 110.

Dobrzynski, Judith. "A New Strain of Merger Mania." *Business Week* (March 21, 1988): 124.

Dorfman, Dan. "Debunking Buyout Talk." *USA Today* (October 6, 1989): B–2.

Drtina, Ralph E., and Marshall R. Gunsel. "Evaluating ESOPs: Spreading Risks and Ensuring Employee Acceptance." *SAM Advanced Management Journal* 53/1 (Winter 1988): 43–48.

Drucker, Peter F. "Corporate Takeovers—What Is to Be Done?" *Public Interest* 82 (Winter 1986).

Dunn, Michael. "Corporate Finance." *Barron's* (February 24, 1988): 39.

Farrell, Christopher. "Investors Can Still Profit from the Merger Game." *Business Week* (November 24, 1986): 97.

Frederickson, James W., Donald C. Hambreck, and Sara Baumron. "A Model of CEO Dismissal." *Academy of Management Review* (September 1988).

Friedman, Jon. "Takeover Stocks: No, the Good Ones Aren't All Taken." *Business Week* (December 26, 1988): 110, 114.

Fromson, Bret Duval. "Life after Debt: How LBOs Do It." *Fortune* 119 (March 1989): 91–92.

Gannes, Stuart. "America's Fastest-Growing Companies." *Fortune* (May 23, 1988): 28–31.

Gilder, George. "New Breed of Innovator." *Success* (September 1988).

Gleckman, Howard. "The SEC Makes Its Move on Drexel and Milken." *Business Week* (September 19, 1988): 32.

Goodrich, Jonathan N. "Privatization in America." *Business Horizons* (January–February 1988): 11–14.

Graef, S. Crystal, and Fred K. Foulkes. "Don't Bail out Underwater Options." *Fortune* 117 (March 14, 1988): 171–2.

Green, Wayne E. "Confusion over Merger-Disclosure Law." *Wall Street Journal* (June 24, 1988).

Greenwald, John. "The Popular Game of Going Private." *Time* (November 4, 1985): 54–55.

Grimm, Robert. "Mergers." *Forbes* (September 12, 1984): 68.

Hamilton, Joan O'C. "Levi Strauss Wants to Be a Family Affair Again." *Business Week* (July 29, 1985): 28.

Harding, Susan D., Leon Hanouille, Joseph C. Rue, and Ara C. Volkan. "Why LBOs Are Popular." *Management Accounting* (December 1985): 51–56.

Harshbarger, Dwight. "Takeover: A Tale of Loss, Change, and Growth." *Executive* (November 1987): 339–43.

Hemming, Richard, and Ali M. Mansor. "Is Privatization the Answer?" *Finance and Development* (September 1988): 31.

Henkoff, Ronald. "Deals of the Year." *Fortune* (January 30, 1989): 162–70.

Hershman, Arlen. "Insider Trading—Why It Can't Be Stopped." *Duns Business Monthly* (June 1984): 52.

Herzel, Leo, and Leo Katz. "Insider Trading: Who Loses?" *Lloyds Book Review* (July 1987): 15.

Hirschoff, Ranlam. "The Privatization Drive." *Africa Report* (July–August 1986): 86–92.

Jaffe, Charles A. "Success by Surprise." *Nation's Business* (September 1989): 30–32.

Jemison, David B., and Sim B. Sitkin. "Acquisitions—The Process Can Be a Problem." *Harvard Business Review* (March–April 1986): 109.

Kadle, David. "Buyout Craze May Be Too Good to Last." *USA Today* (September 30, 1988).

Karmin, Monroe W. "Mergers Give U.S. Industry Tougher Skin." *U.S. News and World Report* (July 8, 1985): 47.

Karp, Irwin. "Let's Look Much Harder at Mergers." *Publishers Weekly* (April 17, 1987): 18.

Kilderie, Ted. "What Do We Mean by Privatization?" *Society* (September–October 1987): 46–51.

King, Resa. "Takeovers Are Back but Now the Frenzy Is Gone." *Business Week* (February 1989): 24–25.

Kirkland, Richard I., Jr. "Merger Mania Is Sweeping Europe." *Fortune International* (December 19, 1988): 42.

Kotkin, Joel. "The Smart Team at Compaq Computer." *INC* (February 1986): 48–56.

———. "What I Do in Private Is My Own Business." *INC* (November 1986): 66–81.

Krusekopf, Charles C. "Pushing Corporate Boards to Be Better." *Fortune* (July 18, 1988).

Lappen, Alyssa A. "Scuffle in the Boardroom." *Forbes* (October 16, 1989): 112.

Larson, Peter. "Former Workers Primed to Buy Closed Alcoa Plant." *Dallas Times Herald* (December 25, 1983): A–39.

Lawes, Murphy. "Are LBO Banks about to Crash?" *Bankers Monthly* 106 (April 1989): 24–28.

Lefkoe, Morty. "Why So Many Mergers Fail." *Fortune* (July 20, 1987): 116.

Levy, David T. "The Transactions Cost Approach to Vertical Integration: An

Empirical Examination." *Review of Economics and Statistics* (August 1985): 439.

Lew, Albert Y. "Mergers and Acquisitions—Growth and Limitations." *National Public Accountant* (October 1989): 26–30.

Lewis, Ralph F. "What Should Audit Committees Do?" *Harvard Business Review* (May–June 1978): 22, 26, 172, 174.

Liberman, Willi. "Power to the People." *Canadian Business Review* (February 1989): 17–19.

Lieberman, David. "Time's Counterattack Is Drawing Acid Reviews." *Business Week* (July 3, 1989): 27–28.

Liebtag, Bill. "Privatizing America." *Journal of Accountancy* (April 1988): 48–52.

Lowestein, Louis. "Management Buyouts." *Columbia Law Review* 85 (1983): 732.

Lublin, Joann S., and Craig Forman. "Ford Snares Jaguar, but $2.5 Billion Is High Price for Prestige." *Wall Street Journal* (November 3, 1989): 1.

McComas, Maggie. "Life Isn't Easy." *Fortune* (December 9, 1985): 43–47.

McConnell, Nancy. "Mergers and Acquisitions." *Fortune* (January 2, 1989).

McMahon, Wm. Franklin. "How Signode's Managers Turned into Entrepreneurs." *Business Week* (June 6, 1983): 86–88.

Madding, Michael. "Big Is Not Better." *Nation* (December 28, 1985): 699.

Marks, Mitchell Lee. "Merging Human Resources." *Merger and Acquisition Magazine* (Summer 1982): 39.

Martz, Larry. "True Greed." *Newsweek* (December 1, 1986): 48–52.

Mercer, Robert. "Raiders Might Be after Your Company Next." *Industry Week* (June 29, 1987): 14.

Michel, Allen, and Israel Shaked. "Evaluating Merger Performance." *California Management Review* (Spring 1985): 109.

Millward, Robert. "The Comparative Performance of Public and Private Ownership." In *The Mixed Economy*, ed. E. Roll, pp. 58–93. London: Macmillan, 1982.

Mitchell, Russell, and Pete Engardio. "But Can He Handle an Ax?" *Business Week* (January 25, 1988): 35.

Modik, Stanley J. "Privatization Push to Stumble." *Industry Week* (July 3, 1989): 54–57.

Moe, Richard C. "Exploring the Limits of Privatization." *Public Administration Review* (November–December 1987): 453.

Moore, Thomas. "How the 12 Top Raiders Rate." *Fortune* (September 28, 1987): 44–54.

Murray, Thomas. "Here Come the 'Tin' Parachute." *Dun's Business Monthly* (January 1987): 62.

Myers, Henry F. "Will Mergers Help or Hurt in the Long Run?" *Wall Street Journal* (May 2, 1988).

Newcomb, Peter. "No One Is Safe." *Forbes* (July 13, 1987): 121.

Nussbaum, Bruce. "Deal Mania—The Tempo Is Frantic and the Prosperity of the U.S. Is at Stake." *Business Week* (November 24, 1986): 75.

Pauly, David. "Merger Inc." *Newsweek* (December 9, 1985): 47.

Perry, Martin K., and Robert H. Groff. "Resale Price Maintenance and Forward Integration into a Monopolistically Competitive Industry." *Quarterly Journal of Economics* (November 1985).

Poole, Claire, and Jeffrey A. Trachtenberg. "Bear Hug." *Forbes* (November 16, 1987): 187.

Powell, Bill, and Rich Thomas. "The Raider: A Quick Fall from Grace." *Newsweek* (December 8, 1986): 66.

Ramirez, Anthony. "What LBOs Really Do to R&D Spending." *Fortune* (March 1989): 98.

Reich, Robert B. "Leveraged Buyouts: America Pays the Price." *New York Times* (January 29, 1989): 32–40.

Reilly, Ann. "Inside Crackdown." *Fortune* (May 14, 1984): 143–44.

Richman, James D. "Merger Decision Making: An Ethical Analysis and Recommendation." *California Management Review* (Fall 1984): 177.

Richman, Tom. "The Entrepreneurial Mystique." *INC* (October 1985): 36.

Ronk, Cheryl O. "The Growing Interest in Privatization." *USA Today* (January 1989): 30–32.

Root, Franklin R. *International Trade and Investment.* (Cincinnati: South-Western, 1973), p. 529.

Rosen, Corey. "A Close-Up View of ESOPs." *Foundary M & T* (September 1986): 32.

Rosen, Corey, and Michael Quarry. "How Well Is Employee Ownership Working." *Harvard Business Review* (September–October 1987): 126.

Russel, George. "Going after the Crooks." *Time* (December 1986): 49.

Samuelson, Robert J. "The Irony of Capitalism." *Newsweek* (January 9, 1989): 44.

Sauerhaft, Stan. "The Mergers of Today." *Business Week* (October 12, 1984): 351.

Scheibla, Shirley. "Split in the SEC." *Barron's* (May 2, 1983): 48–49.

Schiller, Zachery. "Uniroyal: The Road from Giant to Corporate Shell." *Business Week* (July 14, 1986): 29.

Scott, Randy. "Mergers & Acquisitions." *Forbes* (June 2, 1988): 59.

Sease, Douglas K. "Analysts Wonder If Takeover Pace Will Continue." *Wall Street Journal* (April 25, 1988).

Simon, Ruth. "Of Pots and Paintbrushes." *Forbes* (November 3, 1986): 110.

Spragins, Ellyn E. "Leveraged Buyouts Aren't Just for Daredevils Anymore." *Business Week* (August 11, 1986): 50.

Stern, Richard. "The Inside Inside Story." *Forbes* (March 12, 1984): 62–63.

Stratford, Sherman P. "Pushing Corporate Boards to Be Better." *Managing* 118 (July 1988): 60.

Szabo, Joan C. "Small-Business Update." *Nation's Business* 76 (June 1988).

Tidwell, Gary L., and Abdul Aziz. "Insider Trading: How Well Do You Understand the Current Status of the Law?" *California Management Review* (Summer 1988): 117.

Tigner, Brooks. "Brussels Drafting One-Stop Shopping Rules for Growing Wave of European Takeovers." *International Management* (October 1988).

Tricker, R. I. "Improving the Board's Effectiveness." *Journal of General Management* (Spring 1987): 460.

Tully, Shawn. "Europe Goes Wild over Privatization." *Fortune* (March 2, 1987): 68–70.

Turpin-Forster, Shela C. "ESOPs Mean Business." *ABA Banking Journal* (October 1985): 164.

Wallace, Anise C. "Merger Activity Accelerating." *New York Times* (April 11, 1989): 24.

Weidenbaum, Murry. "At the Federal Level in Particular . . ." *Industry Week* (July 3, 1989): 56.

Weinstein, Edward. "Why I Bought the Company." *Journal of Business Strategy* (January–February 1989): 5.

Weiss, Gary. "ABC's of LBOs: What Makes Leveraged Buyouts Popular." *Barron's* (August 19, 1985).

Welles, Chris. "Just How Damning Is the Case Against Drexel Burnham." *Business Week* (November 28, 1988): 61.

———. "Just How Corrupt Is Wall Street." *Business Week* (January 9, 1989): 35.

Wermeil, Stephen. "Supreme Court Declines to Review Law in Wisconsin Curbing Hostile Takeovers." *Wall Street Journal* (November 7, 1989): 6–17.

Work, Clemens P., and Manuel Schiffres. "Leveraged Buyouts—Are They Growing Too Risky?" *U.S. News and World Report* (November 18, 1985): 49–52.

Worthy, Ford. "Money and Markets." *Fortune* (December 22, 1986): 27–29.

Wortzel, Lawrence. "Privatizing Does Not Always Work." *New York Times* (February 14, 1988): 2.

Wyatt, Oscar S., Jr., "Acquisitions: Everyone Can and Should Benefit." *Industry Week* (September 30, 1985): 14.

Yang, C., and J. Weber. "Is Delaware about to Harpoon the Sharks?" *Business Week* (January 25, 1988): 34.

Yong, Catherine. "The New Tax Angle in the Merger Game." *Business Week* (March 21, 1988): 138.

BOOKS

Aharoni, Yair. *The Evolution and Management of State Owned Enterprises*. Hagerstown, Md.: Harper and Row, 1987.

Alkhafaji, Abbass F. *A Stakeholder Approach to Corporate Governance: Managing in a Dynamic Environment*. New York: Quorum, 1989.

Barry, Vincent. *Moral Issues in Business*. 3d ed. Belmont, Calif.: Wadsworth, 1986.

Boyd, Thomas, and S. Winton Korn. *Accounting for Management Planning and Decision Making*. New York: Wiley, 1969.

Bucholz, Rogene A. *Business Environment and Public Policy: Implications for Management and Strategy Formulation*. 3d ed. Englewood Cliffs, N.J.: Prentice-Hall, 1989.

Buckley, Peter J. *The Future of the Multinational Enterprise*. New York: Holmes and Meier, 1976.

Cateora, Philip R. *Marketing: An International Perspective*. Englewood Cliffs, N.J.: Prentice-Hall, 1971.

Clausen, W. *The Development Challenge of the Eighties*. Washington, D.C.: International Bank for Reconstruction and Development, 1986.

Coyne, John. *Management Buyouts*. New York: Croomhelm, 1985.

Czinkota, Michael R., Pietra Rivoli, and Ikka A. Ronkainen. *International Business*. Chicago: Dryden, 1989.

Harrigan, Kathryn R. *Strategic Flexibility*. Lexington, Mass.: Lexington Books, 1985.

Harris, Louis. "Public Sees More Harm Than Good in Corporate Takeovers." *Harris Poll* (February 10–14, 1980), p. 14.

Hax, Arnoldo, and Nicolas Majluf. *Strategic Management: An Integrative Perspective.* Engelwood Cliffs, N.J.: Prentice-Hall, 1984.

Held, Virginia. *Property, Profits, and Economic Justice.* Belmont, Calif.: Wadsworth, 1980).

Herzberg, Frederick. *One More Time: How Do You Motivate Employees?* 3d ed. Plano, Tex.: Business Publications, 1986.

Hooper, John W., et al. *The Law of Business Organizations in East and Central Africa.* Nairobi: East African Literature Bureau, 1976.

Lever, Harold Christopher Hune. *Debt and Danger: The World Financial Crisis.* New York: Atlantic Monthly, 1986.

Mace, Myles L. *Director: Myth and Reality.* Boston: Harvard College, 1971.

Savas, E. S. *Privatizing the Public Sector.* Chatham, N.J.: Chatham House, 1982.

Scharf, Charles A. *Acquisitions, Mergers, Sales, and Takeovers: A Handbook with Forms.* Englewood Cliffs, N.J.: Prentice-Hall, 1971.

Singh, Ajit. *Takeover.* London: Cambridge University Press, 1971.

Sorrell, M. Mathes. *The Smaller Company's Board of Directors.* Conference Board, 1967.

Steiner, Peter O. *Mergers.* Ann Arbor: University of Michigan Press, 1975.

Stemp, Isay. *Corporate Growth Strategies.* American Management Association, 1970.

U.S. Agency for International Development. *Implementing A.I.D. Privatization Objectives.* Washington, D.C., 1986.

Walstedt, Bertil. *State Manufacturing Enterprise in a Mixed Economy: The Turkish Case.* Baltimore: Johns Hopkins University Press, 1980.

Wheelen, Thomas L. *Strategic Management and Business Policy.* New York: Addison-Wesley, 1986.

Woods, Gordon. *The Acquisition Decision.* National Association of Accountants, 1985.

INDEX

About the Author

ABBASS F. ALKHAFAJI is Associate Professor of Management at Slippery Rock University. His previous works include *A Stakeholder Approach to Corporate Governance* (Quorum, 1989), and he is co-author of *International Management Challenge*. He is the editor of the *International Academy of Management and Marketing Proceedings, Management Magazine,* and *International Consumer Marketing News.*